Leveled Practice for the Virginia Standards of Learning Assessment

Grade 2

Harcourt

Orlando   Austin   Chicago   New York   Toronto   London   San Diego

Visit *The Learning Site!*
www.harcourtschool.com

ISBN 0-15-326260-5

2 3 4 5 6 7 8 9 10   082   10 09 08 07 06 05 04 03 02

Contents

Tips for Taking a Test

Be Prepared

1. Sit up straight in your chair.
2. Keep your eyes on the teacher and on the test booklet.
3. Have your sharpened pencils ready.

Circle Your Answers

Mark your answers carefully when you take a test. Draw a complete circle around the letter beside your answer choice. Look at this example.

1 **When I mark an answer, I should —**

   A draw a line through the letter.

   Ⓑ circle the letter.

   C make a check beside the letter.

   D circle the whole answer choice.

Follow Directions

Take time to read test directions carefully. Think about what the directions ask you to do. Read the example directions below. Then answer the question.

DIRECTIONS

Read the story. Then read each question about the story. Circle the letter of the best answer.

1 **What should you do after you read the story?**

   A Answer the hardest question first.

   B Read the story two more times.

   C Read each question about the story.

   D Go on to the next story.

Read the Questions

Sometimes a word in a test question has all capital letters or a line under it. Paying attention to that word will help you answer the question correctly. Read the sample test questions below. Then answer the questions that go with each one.

Which words from lines 12 through 15 are the names of THINGS?

1 **What is the important word in this test question?**

   A things

   B through

   C lines

   D words

What does the word <u>investigated</u> mean in paragraph 2 of the story?

2 **What is the important word in this test question?**

   A story

   B paragraph

   C mean

   D investigated

After you read a test question, think about what you must know to answer it. Ask yourself, "What is this question really asking?" Read the sample test question below. Then answer the question below it.

Another good title for this story is —

   A "Baseball Greats."

   B "Women's Basketball."

   C "The Best Batters."

   D "Baseball's Most Famous Pitchers."

1 **What is this test question really asking about the story?**

   A What is the topic of the story?

   B What event happens first?

   C Who is the main character?

   D What is the author's point of view?

The Mixed-Up Chameleon

➡ **Read the paragraph. Then choose the best answer to each question.**

A Visit to the Pet Shop

On Saturdays, Pete goes to the pet shop. He likes to see the fish. He likes to see the rabbits. He gets a treat for his pet chameleon. Pete has a baby brother. Pete likes to start his weekend this way!

Example: **Which sentence does not belong in the paragraph?**

   A He likes to see the fish.

   Ⓑ Pete has a baby brother.

   C Pete likes to start his weekend this way!

   D He gets a treat for his pet chameleon.

1 What is the main idea of this paragraph?

   A Pete has a pet chameleon that changes colors.

   B Pete wants to buy a fish from the pet shop.

   C On Saturdays, Pete goes to the pet shop.

   D Pete takes good care of his pet chameleon.

> **COACH** **Tip**
> Reread the first sentence of the paragraph. It often tells the main idea.

2 What sentence from the paragraph tells more about the main idea?

   F Chameleons have long tongues.

   G On Sundays, Pete likes to go for long bike rides.

   H Pete likes to start his weekend this way!

   J Pete helps take care of his family's dog.

> **COACH** **Tip**
> Think about the main idea as you read each answer choice.

The Mixed-Up Chameleon

 Read the paragraph. Then choose the best answer to each question.

A Visit to the Pet Shop

On Saturdays, Pete goes to the pet shop. He likes to see the fish swim. He likes to see the rabbits. Once, Pete got to hold a baby rabbit. Its fur was very soft. Pete always buys a treat for his pet chameleon. He has a baby brother named John. Pete thinks this is a great way to start his weekend!

---

1 What is the main idea of this paragraph? ——— COACH **Tip**

- **A** Pete has a pet chameleon that changes colors.

- **B** Pete wants to buy a fish from the pet shop.

- **C** On Saturdays, Pete goes to the pet shop.

- **D** Pete takes good care of his pet chameleon.

> Look for the sentence that tells what the paragraph is about.

2 Which sentence does not belong in the paragraph?

- **F** He likes to see the fish swim.

- **G** He has a baby brother named John.

- **H** Pete thinks this is a great way to start his weekend!

- **J** Pete always buys a treat for his pet chameleon.

3 What sentence from the paragraph tells more about the main idea?

- **A** Chameleons catch their food with long tongues.

- **B** On Sundays, Pete likes to go for long bike rides.

- **C** Pete thinks this is a great way to start his weekend!

- **D** Pete helps take care of his family's dog.

Name _____   **The Mixed-Up Chameleon**

➡️ **Read the paragraph. Then choose the best answer to each question.**

A Visit to the Pet Shop

Every Saturday, Pete visits the pet shop. He likes to watch the fish swim. He likes the tropical fish best of all. Pete likes to watch the rabbits, too. Once, the owner of the pet shop let Pete hold a baby rabbit. Its fur was soft, and its heart beat very fast. Pete always buys a treat for his pet chameleon. He has a baby brother named John. Pete thinks this is a great way to start his weekend!

---

1 What is the main idea of this paragraph?

   A Pete has a pet chameleon that changes colors.

   B Pete wants to buy a fish from the pet shop.

   C On Saturdays, Pete goes to the pet shop.

   D Pete takes good care of his pet chameleon.

2 Which sentence does not belong in the paragraph?

   F He likes to watch the fish swim.

   G He has a baby brother named John.

   H Pete thinks this is a great way to start his weekend!

   J Pete always buys a treat for his pet chameleon.

3 What sentence from the paragraph tells more about the main idea?

   A Chameleons zap their food with long tongues.

   B On Sundays, Pete likes to go for long bike rides.

   C Pete thinks this is a great way to start his weekend!

   D Pete helps take care of his family's dog.

Theme 1 – Reading A   **3**

Get Up and Go!

➡️ **Find the word that has the same sound as the underlined letters in the first word.**

Example: <u>sa</u>me

    A come

    B sake

    C small

    Ⓓ came

1 <u>ra</u>ke

    A blame

    B brake

    C ballgame

    D rain

> **COACH Tip**
> Say each word softly to yourself. Listen for a word that rhymes with the first word.

2 <u>fr</u>ame

    F shake

    G shade

    H shout

    J shame

3 <u>g</u>ame

    A seven

    B brake

    C lake

    D blame

> **COACH Tip**
> Read the first word carefully. Be sure you know the sound the underlined letters stand for.

4 <u>fla</u>ke

    F tame

    G flat

    H flame

    J take

Get Up and Go!

➡️ **Find the word that has the same sound as the underlined letters in the first word.**

1 r<u>ake</u>

  A blame

  B brake

  C ballgame

  D rain

2 f<u>ra</u>me

  F shake

  G shade

  H shout

  J shame

3 <u>game</u>

  A seven

  B brake

  C lake

  D blame

4 fl<u>ake</u>

  F tame

  G flat

  H flame

  J take

5 <u>came</u>

  A coin

  B cake

  C lame

  D leak

COACH Tip

Look at the underlined part of the word. Listen for its sound as you say each choice softly to yourself.

© Harcourt

Name _____

 Find the word that has the same sound as the underlined letters in the first word.

1 r<u>a</u>ke

A blame

B brake

C ballgame

D rain

2 fr<u>ame</u>

F shake

G shade

H shout

J shame

3 <u>game</u>

A seven

B brake

C lake

D blame

4 fl<u>ake</u>

F tame

G flat

H flame

J take

5 c<u>ame</u>

A coin

B cake

C lame

D leak

6 handsh<u>ake</u>

F makeup

G handsome

H maintain

J hardly

7 f<u>ame</u>

A farmer

B nickname

C noodle

D families

8 mist<u>ake</u>

F kittens

G bakeshop

H everyday

J stacks

9 sh<u>ame</u>ful

A rename

B members

C milkshake

D return

10 ballg<u>ame</u>

F basketball

G otherwise

H bellyache

J overcame

➡ **Find the word in which the letters *ed* have the same sound as they have in the first word.**

Example: drif<u>ed</u>

    A backed

    Ⓑ floated

    C soaked

    D locked

1 work<u>ed</u>

    A needed

    B mailed

    C sipped

    D sorted

> **COACH Tip**
>
> Say each word softly to yourself. Find the word that ends with the "t" sound.

2 pull<u>ed</u>

    F waited

    G picked

    H rushed

    J hugged

3 pain<u>ed</u>

    A landed

    B doomed

    C opened

    D finished

> **COACH Tip**
>
> Find the word that ends with the "id" sound.

4 rain<u>ed</u>

    F knitted

    G reached

    H played

    J snacked

Find the word in which the letters *ed* have the same sound as they have in the first word.

1 work<u>ed</u>

   A needed

   B mailed

   C sipped

   D sorted

2 pull<u>ed</u>

   F waited

   G picked

   H rushed

   J hugged

 Tip

Remember that the letters *ed* can stand for the "t" sound, the "id" sound, or the "d" sound.

3 paint<u>ed</u>

   A landed

   B doomed

   C opened

   D finished

4 rain<u>ed</u>

   F knitted

   G reached

   H played

   J snacked

5 pass<u>ed</u>

   A laughed

   B poured

   C littered

   D panted

➡️ Find the word in which the letters *ed* have the same sound as they have in the first word.

1 work<u>ed</u>

   A needed

   B mailed

   C sipped

   D sorted

2 pull<u>ed</u>

   F waited

   G picked

   H rushed

   J hugged

3 paint<u>ed</u>

   A landed

   B doomed

   C opened

   D finished

4 rain<u>ed</u>

   F knitted

   G reached

   H played

   J snacked

5 pass<u>ed</u>

   A laughed

   B poured

   C littered

   D panted

6 head<u>ed</u>

   F sailed

   G wanted

   H wished

   J seemed

7 loop<u>ed</u>

   A strengthened

   B stranded

   C strayed

   D stacked

8 wagg<u>ed</u>

   F ringed

   G roosted

   H flocked

   J rented

9 hunt<u>ed</u>

   A trapped

   B learned

   C turned

   D loaded

10 enter<u>ed</u>

   F floated

   G followed

   H packed

   J printed

Days With Frog and Toad

  Read the paragraph. Then choose the best answer to each question.

Two Good Cooks

I have two sisters. Both of them love to cook. Holly likes to make salads. Jane likes to bake cakes. Holly is a messy cook. Jane is a neat cook. My sisters like cooking different foods. Each likes to eat what the other cooks. So do I!

Example: Who likes to make salads?

     Ⓐ Holly

     B Jane

     C Holly and Jane

     D Holly and Jane's brother

1 What is the same about Holly and Jane?

     A They like to wash dishes.

     B They both like to bake cakes.

     C They are both messy cooks.

     D They both love to cook.

 Tip

Look for the word *both* in the paragraph. It tells you that two things are the same.

2 What is different about Holly and Jane?

     F They like to cook.

     G They like to eat each other's cooking.

     H Holly is messy, and Jane is neat.

     J They are sisters.

Tip

Skip the answer choices that tell how the sisters are the same.

Days With Frog and Toad

➡ **Read the paragraph. Then choose the best answer to each question.**

Two Good Cooks

I have two sisters named Holly and Jane. Both my sisters love to cook. Holly likes to make salads filled with vegetables. Jane likes to bake cakes with fruit. Holly is a messy cook. Jane is a neat cook. My sisters like cooking different foods, but each likes to eat what the other cooks. So do I!

1 What is the same about Holly and Jane?

 Tip

The word *both* is a clue that two things are the same.

    A They like to wash dishes.

    B They both like to bake cakes.

    C They are both messy cooks.

    D They both love to cook.

2 What is different about Holly and Jane?

    F They like to cook.

    G They like to eat each other's cooking.

    H Holly is messy, but Jane is neat.

    J They are sisters in the same family.

3 Where is one place that both Holly and Jane like to be?

    A in the living room

    B in the kitchen

    C in the backyard

    D in the library

Days With Frog and Toad

➡ **Read the paragraph. Then choose the best answer to each question.**

Two Good Cooks

I have two sisters. Both my sisters love to cook. Holly likes to make healthful salads filled with vegetables. Jane likes to bake delicious cakes topped with fruit. Holly is a messy cook. When she cooks, the sink is piled high with dirty dishes. Jane is a neat cook. She cleans up as she goes along. My sisters like cooking different foods, but they enjoy eating each other's cooking. So do I!

1 What is the same about Holly and Jane?

  A They like to wash dishes.

  B They both like to bake cakes.

  C They are both messy cooks.

  D They both love to cook.

2 What is different about Holly and Jane?

  F They like to cook.

  G They like to eat each other's cooking.

  H Holly is messy, but Jane is neat.

  J They are sisters in the same family.

3 Where is one place that both Holly and Jane like to be?

  A in the living room

  B in the kitchen

  C in the backyard

  D in the library

Wilson Sat Alone

➡️ **Read the story. Then choose the best answer to each question.**

Austin Makes a Friend

Austin stopped. He saw the house with the mean dog. His heart beat fast. His legs shook. He could hear the dog barking. Austin got ready to run. Then he saw the new girl in his class.

"Hi," she said. "Come meet my dog. Lucky loves to bark, but he's very nice."

Austin smiled and walked over to meet Lucky.

Example: What is the setting of this story?

     A   a beach

     B   the woods

     Ⓒ   a neighborhood

     D   a hospital

1 How does Austin feel at the beginning of the story?

     A   frightened

     B   angry

     C   sad

     D   tired

 Tip

Reread the first few sentences. Think about how you would feel if your heart beat fast and your legs shook.

2 How does Austin feel at the end of the story?

     F   nervous

     G   bored

     H   hungry

     J   happy

 Tip

Reread the ending of the story. Look for clues that tell how Austin feels.

Wilson Sat Alone

➡ **Read the story. Then choose the best answer to each question.**

Austin Makes a Friend

Austin looked down the block. He could see the house with the mean dog. His heart beat faster, and his legs began to shake. Just then the dog started barking. Austin got ready to run. Suddenly, the new girl in his class came out.

"Hi," she said. "Come meet my dog. Lucky has a loud bark, but he's very nice."

Austin walked over to the fence. He smiled and asked to pet Lucky.

---

1 How does Austin feel at the beginning of the story?

  A frightened

  B angry

  C sad

  D tired

2 How does Austin feel at the end of the story?

  F nervous

  G bored

  H hungry

  J happy

3 Why do Austin's feelings change?

  A He sees that the dog is tied up.

  B He learns that the dog is friendly.

  C He knows that he can run fast.

  D He learns the dog's name.

COACH Tip

Reread the first few sentences. Think about how Austin acts. Look for clues that tell how Austin feels.

© Harcourt

➡ **Read the story. Then choose the best answer to each question.**

Austin Makes a Friend

Austin looked down the block. He had almost reached the house with the fierce dog. He could feel his heart speed up, and his legs begin to tremble. Just then the dog began to bark. Austin got ready to run. Suddenly, the new girl in his class appeared on the porch.

"Hi, Austin," she said. "Come meet Lucky. He has a loud bark, but he's very gentle." Austin walked over to the fence. He smiled as he petted Lucky.

---

1 How does Austin feel at the beginning of the story?

   A frightened

   B angry

   C sad

   D tired

2 How does Austin feel at the end of the story?

   F nervous

   G bored

   H hungry

   J happy

3 Why do Austin's feelings change?

   A He sees that the dog is tied up.

   B He learns that the dog is friendly.

   C He knows that he can run fast.

   D He learns the dog's name.

Theme 1 Writing

 Howard wants to write a letter to his friend Chad. He wants to tell Chad about his class play. Howard made this web to help him write the letter. Use it to answer questions 1 and 2.

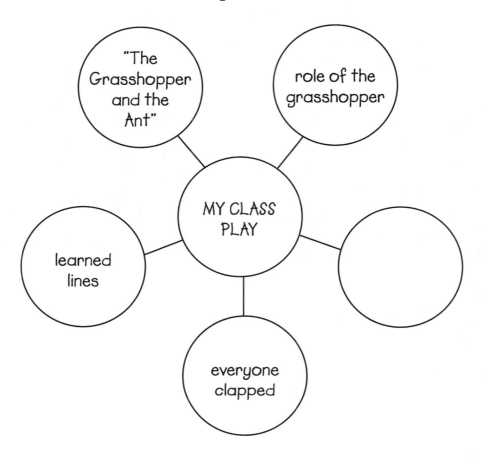

1 Which of these could Howard add to the web?

   A play soccer after school

   B children and parents came

   C mail the letter at the post office

   D finish math homework

2 This web will help Howard to —

   F plan what to write in his letter.

   G find out if people liked the play.

   H think of things that happen at school.

   J learn his lines.

Here is the first part of Howard's draft. Use it to answer questions 3, 4, and 5.

October 14, 2002

Dear Chad,

   (1) I want to tell you about my class play. (2) It was the story of "The Grasshopper and the Ant." (3) I played the part of the grasshopper. (4) I saw a grasshopper by my house. (5) I worked hard to learn all my lines.

---

3 Which sentence tells the main idea of Howard's letter?

   A 1

   B 3

   C 4

   D 5

4 Which sentence does not belong in Howard's letter?

   F 1

   G 2

   H 4

   J 5

5 Which sentence might Howard add to the beginning of the letter to make it sound more friendly?

   A Please read this letter slowly.

   B I like to write only about myself

   C How are you doing?

   D I am writing to give you information.

Read the next part of Howard's draft and answer the questions. This part has underlined words. The questions ask about the underlined words.

---

(6) All the children in the second grade came to see our class play. (7) Some moms and dads <u>came, too?</u> (8) At the end of the <u>play. everyone</u> clapped. (9) It made me feel good.

<u>Your friend</u>

Howard

---

6 In sentence 7, <u>came, too?</u> should be written —

  A   came, too.

  B   Came, too.

  C   Came, too?

  D   came, too?

7 In sentence 8, <u>play. everyone</u> should be written —

  F   play. Everyone

  G   play, everyone

  H   play? everyone

  J   as it is

8 How should <u>Your friend</u> be written?

  A   You're friend

  B   Your friend:

  C   Your friend,

  D   Your friend.

Name _____ **The Enormous Turnip**

➡ **Read the paragraph. Then choose the best answer to each question.**

Making Applesauce

Every fall, Mr. Lewis makes applesauce. He uses the apples from his enormous apple tree. First he picks the apples. Next he washes them. Then he cuts up the apples. After that he cooks them. Finally he mashes the apples and pushes them through a strainer. The applesauce is ready to eat.

Example: **What does Mr. Lewis do first?**

    A He washes the apples.

    B He cuts up the apples.

    C He pushes the apples through a strainer.

    Ⓓ He picks the apples.

 Tip
> The words that tell when something happened are important. Look for a sentence that has the word *first*.

1 What does Mr. Lewis do after he washes the apples?

    A He cuts up the apples.

    B He pushes the apples through a strainer.

    C He mashes the apples.

    D He cooks the apples.

2 What is the last thing Mr. Lewis does before the applesauce is ready?

Tip
> Look for a sentence that has the word *finally*.

    F He cuts up the apples.

    G He pushes the apples through a strainer.

    H He washes the apples.

    J He cooks the apples.

The Enormous Turnip

 Read the paragraph. Then choose the best answer to each question.

Making Applesauce

Every fall, Mr. Lewis makes applesauce. He uses the apples from his enormous apple tree. First he uses a ladder to pick the apples. Next he washes the apples to get rid of dirt. Then he cuts up the apples. After that he cooks the pieces until they are soft. Finally Mr. Lewis mashes the apples and pushes them through a strainer. This gets rid of the seeds. The applesauce is ready to eat.

1 What does Mr. Lewis do first?

As you read, look for time-order words. Choose the one answer that tells what happens first.

   A He washes the apples.

   B He cuts up the apples.

   C He pushes the apples through a strainer.

   D He picks the apples.

2 What does Mr. Lewis do after he washes the apples?

   F He cuts up the apples.

   G He pushes the apples through a strainer.

   H He mashes the apples.

   J He cooks the apples.

3 What is the last thing that Mr. Lewis does before the applesauce is ready?

   A He cuts up the apples.

   B He pushes the apples through a strainer.

   C He washes the apples.

   D He cooks the apples.

The Enormous Turnip

 Read the paragraph. Then choose the best answer to each question.

Making Applesauce

Every autumn, Mr. Lewis makes applesauce. He uses the apples that grow on his enormous apple tree. First he climbs a tall ladder to pick the apples. Next he carefully washes the apples to remove dirt and insects. Then he cuts the apples into quarters. After that he cooks the pieces in a big pot until they are soft. Finally Mr. Lewis mashes the apples and pushes them through a wire strainer. This gets rid of all the cores and seeds. The applesauce is ready to eat!

1 What does Mr. Lewis do first?

  A He washes the apples.

  B He cuts up the apples.

  C He pushes the apples through a strainer.

  D He picks the apples.

2 What does Mr. Lewis do after he washes the apples?

  F He cuts up the apples.

  G He pushes the apples through a strainer.

  H He mashes the apples.

  J He cooks the apples.

3 What is the last thing that Mr. Lewis does before the applesauce is ready?

  A He cuts up the apples.

  B He pushes the apples through a strainer.

  C He washes the apples.

  D He cooks the apples.

Read the paragraph. Then choose the best answer to each question.

Tara Helps Out

Once a week, Tara helps out in the library after school. She works with Mrs. Rice, the school librarian. One of Tara's jobs is to put books back where they belong. Sometimes she helps get new books ready. Once she and Mrs. Rice hung pictures around the room. Mrs. Rice says that Tara is a big help at the library.

Example: **What is the main idea of this paragraph?**

  A Mrs. Rice is the school librarian.

  Ⓑ Once a week, Tara helps out in the school library.

  C Tara once hung pictures in the school library.

  D Tara puts the library books where they belong.

 Tip
The main idea is what the paragraph is mostly about. The first sentence often tells the main idea.

1 Which sentence below does not tell more about the main idea?

  A Tara likes to read books about helping others.

  B Tara does many different jobs in the library.

  C Tara helps to get new books ready.

  D Mrs. Rice is happy to have Tara's help.

2 Which sentence could you add to tell more about the main idea?

  F Each library book must have a card.

  G Tara walks home at four o'clock.

  H Last year, Tara helped plant flowers in the school garden.

  J Tara helps put new covers on old books.

 Tip
Look for a sentence that you would expect to find in the paragraph.

➡ **Read the paragraph. Then choose the best answer to each question.**

Tara Helps Out

Once a week, Tara helps out in the library after school. One of her jobs is to put books back on the shelves. Tara also puts the picture books in order. Sometimes she helps Mrs. Rice, the school librarian, get new books ready. Once she helped Mrs. Rice hang pictures around the room. Mrs. Rice says that children who give their time like Tara are a big help at the library.

1 What is the main idea of this paragraph? **COACH Tip**

   A Mrs. Rice is the school librarian.

   B Once a week, Tara helps out in the school library.

   C Tara once hung pictures in the school library.

   D Tara puts the library books where they belong.

> The main idea tells the most important idea of a selection. To find the main idea, think about what the paragraph is mostly about.

2 Which sentence does not tell more about the main idea?

   F Tara likes to read books about helping others.

   G Tara does many different jobs in the library.

   H Tara helps to get new books ready.

   J Mrs. Rice is happy to have Tara's help.

3 Which sentence could you add to tell more about the main idea?

   A Each library book must have a card.

   B Tara walks home from the library at four o'clock.

   C Last year, Tara helped plant flowers in the school garden.

   D Tara helps put new covers on old books.

Read the paragraph. Then choose the best answer to each question.

Tara Helps Out

Once a week, Tara helps out in the library after school. One of her jobs is to return books to their places on the shelves. Tara also spends time putting the picture books back in alphabetical order. Sometimes she helps Mrs. Rice, the school librarian, cover the new books with plastic. Once she helped Mrs. Rice hang pictures on the bulletin boards. Mrs. Rice says that she depends on the help of volunteers like Tara. They help to keep things running smoothly at the library.

---

1 What is the main idea of this paragraph?

  A Mrs. Rice is the school librarian.

  B Once a week, Tara helps out in the school library.

  C Tara once hung pictures in the school library.

  D Tara puts the library books where they belong.

2 Which sentence does not tell more about the main idea?

  F Tara likes to read books about helping others.

  G Tara does many different jobs in the library.

  H Tara helps to get new books ready.

  J Mrs. Rice is happy to have Tara's help.

3 Which sentence could you add to tell more about the main idea?

  A Each library book must have a card.

  B Tara walks home from the library at four o'clock.

  C Last year, Tara helped plant flowers in the school garden.

  D Tara helps put new covers on old books.

Choose the correct abbreviation for each word.

An abbreviation is the short form of a word. A person's title, the names of days and months, addresses, and measurements are often abbreviated.

Example: **Monday**

    A mon.

    Ⓑ Mon.

    C Mon

    D mon

February						
Sun.	Mon.	Tues.	Wed.	Thur.	Fri.	Sat.
						①
2	3	4	5	6	7	8
9	10	11	12	13	14	15
16	17	18	19	20	21	22
23	24	25	26	27	28	

1 Saturday

    A sat.

    B Sat.

    C Sat

    D sat

2 inch

    F In

    G In.

    H in.

    J in

 Tip

Most abbreviations for measurements do not have capital letters.

3 Avenue

    A Ave.

    B Ave

    C ave.

    D ave

Tip

Remember that most abbreviations end with a period.

Mr. Putter and Tabby Fly the Plane

 Choose the correct abbreviation for each word.

An abbreviation is the short form of a word. A person's title, the names of days and months, addresses, and measurements are often abbreviated.

1 Saturday

   A sat.

   B Sat.

   C Sat

   D sat

2 inch

   F In

   G In.

   H in.

   J in

3 Avenue

   A Ave.

   B Ave

   C ave.

   D ave

4 February

   F Feb

   G Feb.

   H feb.

   J feb

February						
Sun.	Mon.	Tues.	Wed.	Thur.	Fri.	Sat.
						(1)
2	3	4	5	6	7	8
9	10	11	12	13	14	15
16	17	18	19	20	21	22
23	24	25	26	27	28	

 Tip

Remember that most measurement abbreviations do not start with a capital letter.

© Harcourt

Mr. Putter and Tabby Fly the Plane

➡️ **Choose the correct abbreviation for each word.**

An abbreviation is the short form of a word. A person's title, the names of days and months, addresses, and measurements are often abbreviated.

1 Saturday

   A sat.

   B Sat.

   C Sat

   D sat

2 inch

   F In

   G In.

   H in.

   J in

3 Avenue

   A Ave.

   B Ave

   C ave.

   D ave

4 February

   F Feb

   G Feb.

   H feb.

   J feb

5 Mister

   A Mr

   B mr.

   C Mr.

   D mr

6 kilogram

   F kg

   G kg.

   H Kg

   J Kg.

7 Drive

   A dr

   B Dr.

   C dr.

   D Dr

8 Tuesday

   F Tues

   G tues.

   H tues

   J Tues.

© Harcourt

Hedgehog Bakes a Cake

 Read the paragraph. Then choose the best answer to each question.

Cookie Baker

Dan likes to bake cookies. He chooses easy recipes. They are simple to follow. Dan's cookies are big. They are so large that they cover the whole cookie sheet. Everyone thinks Dan's cookies are tasty and delicious. They are so good that they don't last very long.

Example: Which word means the same as <u>big</u>?

    A small

    B slow

    Ⓒ large

    D quiet

1 Which word means the same as <u>easy</u>?

    A simple

    B hard

    C long

    D short

 COACH Tip

> Something that is easy is not difficult. Look for a word that tells that something is not difficult.

2 Which word does NOT mean the same as <u>delicious</u>?

    F good

    G tasty

    H large

    J yummy

COACH Tip

> Read the question carefully. Pay attention to words that have all capital letters.

Read the paragraph. Then choose the best answer to each question.

Cookie Baker

Dan really enjoys baking cookies. He chooses easy recipes that are simple to follow. Dan's cookies are huge. They are so large that only one cookie fits on a cookie sheet.
Dan also likes to make fancy cookies with colorful frosting. Everyone in the family thinks that Dan's cookies are delicious. They are so good that they don't last very long.

---

1 Which word means the same as <u>easy</u>?

  A simple

  B hard

  C long

  D short

COACH **Tip**

Test your choice by putting it in the sentence in place of the word *easy*. The sentence should still have the same meaning.

2 Which word does NOT mean the same as <u>delicious</u>?

  F good

  G tasty

  H large

  J yummy

3 Which word is a synonym for <u>huge</u>?

  A hungry

  B tiny

  C fancy

  D enormous

Name _____

Hedgehog Bakes a Cake

 Read the paragraph. Then choose the best answer to each question.

Cookie Baker

Dan's hobby is baking cookies. He enjoys easy recipes that are simple to follow. Dan's cookies are chewy, moist, and filled with flavor. They are so huge that they cover an entire cookie sheet. Dan also likes to decorate his cookies with colored frosting, nuts, and dried fruit. Everyone in the family thinks that Dan's cookies are delicious. They are so good that they quickly disappear.

1 Which word means the same as <u>easy</u>?

   A simple

   B difficult

   C long

   D short

2 Which word does NOT mean the same as <u>delicious</u>?

   F good

   G tasty

   H large

   J yummy

3 Which word is a synonym for <u>huge</u>?

   A hungry

   B tiny

   C fancy

   D enormous

© Harcourt

Name _____

Lemonade for Sale

 Find the word that has the same sound as the underlined letters in the first word.

Example: ma<u>r</u>k

    A ant

    B candy

    Ⓒ ark

    D cake

1 d<u>ar</u>k

    A dare

    B peek

    C back

    D bark

2 y<u>ar</u>d

    F herd

    G hard

    H heap

    J happy

3 al<u>ar</u>m

    A share

    B brake

    C charm

    D aloud

4 f<u>ar</u>ther

    F car

    G curb

    H careful

    J catch

 Tip

Softly say each answer choice to yourself. Listen for the sound that you hear in the first word.

COACH Tip

Read all the choices before you pick one.

Lemonade for Sale

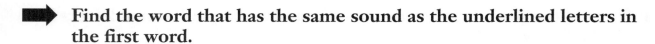

Find the word that has the same sound as the underlined letters in the first word.

1 d<u>ar</u>k

   A dare

   B peek

   C back

   D bark

2 backy<u>ar</u>d

   F herd

   G hard

   H heap

   J happy

> **COACH Tip**
>
> Think about the vowel sound in each word before you mark your answer.

3 al<u>arm</u>ed

   A shared

   B brake

   C charming

   D aloud

4 <u>far</u>ther

   F car

   G curb

   H careful

   J catch

5 l<u>ar</u>k

   A flights

   B freedom

   C shaking

   D sparkle

➡️ **Find the word that has the same sound as the underlined letters in the first word.**

1 d<u>ar</u>k

  A dare

  B peek

  C back

  D bark

2 back<u>yar</u>d

  F herd

  G hard

  H heap

  J happy

3 al<u>arm</u>ed

  A shared

  B brake

  C charming

  D aloud

4 f<u>ar</u>ther

  F car

  G curb

  H careful

  J catch

5 l<u>ark</u>

  A flights

  B freedom

  C shaking

  D sparkle

6 b<u>ar</u>gain

  F change

  G chart

  H chose

  J chain

7 rem<u>ark</u>

  A smear

  B landing

  C looks

  D stark

8 <u>car</u>toon

  F hardball

  G together

  H halfway

  J terrific

9 l<u>ar</u>gest

  A assembly

  B automobile

  C amazement

  D argument

10 <u>ar</u>m<u>or</u>

  F daylight

  G education

  H disarming

  J earthly

Theme 2 Writing

 Kelsey wants to write a story about a girl who helped someone. Kelsey made this map to help her write the story. Use it to answer questions 1 and 2.

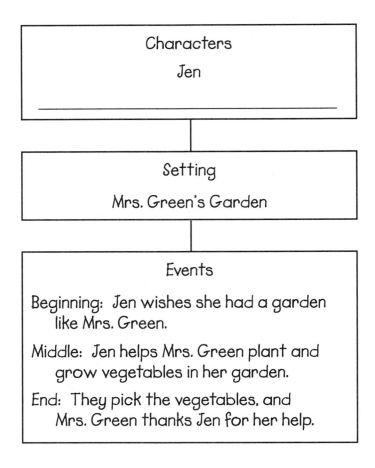

Characters

Jen

_____

Setting

Mrs. Green's Garden

Events

Beginning: Jen wishes she had a garden
   like Mrs. Green.

Middle: Jen helps Mrs. Green plant and
   grow vegetables in her garden.

End: They pick the vegetables, and
   Mrs. Green thanks Jen for her help.

1 This map will help Kelsey to —

   A find out how to plant a garden.

   B plan her story.

   C spell the words in the story.

   D find out how a garden grows.

**2 Which of these could Kelsey add to the map
under <u>Characters</u>?**

   F grow vegetables

   G made vegetable soup

   H happened last year

   J Mrs. Green

34

Here is the first part of Kelsey's draft. Use it to answer the questions.

> (1) Jen saw Mrs. Green in her backyard next door. (2) Mrs. Green was getting ready to plant her garden. (3) Jen wished she had a garden. (4) Got an idea. (5) She asked Mrs. Green if she could help.

3 Which of these could be added after sentence 5?

A Mrs. Green said she would be glad to have Jen's help.

B This is a story about helping.

C Jen has a big garden with lots of vegetables.

D Mrs. Green lives next door to Jen.

4 Which of these is not a complete sentence?

F 1

G 3

H 4

J 5

5 Which sentence tells the problem of the story?

A 1

B 2

C 3

D 4

6 Which two sentences help you decide what the setting is?

F 1 and 4

G 1 and 2

H 3 and 4

J 4 and 5

➡️ **Read the next part of Kelsey's draft and answer the questions. This part has underlined words. The questions ask about the underlined words.**

---

(6) Jen helped <u>dig the erth</u> and plant the seeds. (7) She helped water the garden and <u>pull out weeds</u>. (8) She watched the seeds grow into strong plants.

(9) Jen helped <u>mrs green</u> pick the vegetables when they were ready. (10) Mrs. Green <u>thankd</u> Jen for her help. (11) She gave Jen a basket of vegetables to take home!

---

7 **In sentence 6, <u>dig the erth</u> should be written —**

  A dig the erath

  B dig the earth

  C dug the earth

  D as it is

8 **In sentence 9, <u>mrs green</u> should be written —**

  F Mrs green

  G mrs. Green

  H Mrs. Green

  J Mrs. green

9 **In sentence 10, how should <u>thankd</u> be spelled?**

  A thanked

  B thankedd

  C thankked

  D thaned

Johnny Appleseed

➡️ **Find the word that has the same sound as the underlined letters in the first word.**

Example: d<u>ear</u>

    A hard

   Ⓑ hear

    C dare

    D deal

1 r<u>ear</u>

    A deer

    B care

    C barn

    D card

2 ch<u>eer</u>

    F park

    G chart

    H year

    J chose

3 uncl<u>ear</u>

    A shared

    B yarn

    C stare

    D steer

4 p<u>eer</u>

    F needy

    G nearly

    H known

    J keeps

COACH Tip

Say the word *rear* and listen carefully for the ending sound. Remember that the letters *ear* and *eer* can both stand for the same sound.

➡ **Find the word that has the same sound as the underlined letters in the first word.**

1 r<u>ear</u>

   A deer

   B care

   C barn

   D card

COACH Tip

Remember that the ending sound you hear in the word *rear* can have more than one spelling.

2 ch<u>eer</u>

   F park

   G chart

   H year

   J chose

3 uncl<u>ear</u>

   A shared

   B yarn

   C stare

   D steer

4 p<u>eer</u>

   F needy

   G nearly

   H known

   J keeps

5 volun<u>teer</u>

   A marker

   B appeared

   C stormed

   D alarming

Name _____ **Johnny Appleseed**

➡️ **Find the word that has the same sound as the underlined letters in the first word.**

1 r__ear__

- A deer
- B care
- C barn
- D card

2 ch__ee__r

- F park
- G chart
- H year
- J chose

3 uncl__ear__

- A shared
- B yarn
- C stare
- D steer

4 p__eer__

- F needy
- G nearly
- H known
- J keeps

5 volunt__eer__

- A marker
- B appeared
- C stormed
- D alarming

6 pion__ee__r

- F spear
- G pound
- H speak
- J peach

7 f__ea__rless

- A rarely
- B clearly
- C release
- D closest

8 b__ear__d

- F daughter
- G cheerleader
- H chairwoman
- J dinosaur

9 reind__eer__

- A smart
- B eighteen
- C earthworm
- D smear

10 n__ear__by

- F engineer
- G entrance
- H nervous
- J nephew

From Seed to Plant

  Read the paragraph and the diagram. Then choose the best answer to each question.

Mrs. Jacobs's Garden

Mrs. Jacobs has a big garden. She likes growing plants from seeds. Each part of her garden has one kind of plant.

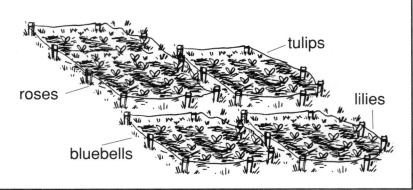

Example: Which flower does Mrs. Jacobs grow the most of?

(A) roses

B tulips

C bluebells

D lilies

1 The diagram tells —

A which plants are in the garden.

B how long the garden is.

C how many years Mrs. Jacobs has gardened.

D which plants need more water.

Look carefully at the diagram. Think about what the words *roses, lilies, bluebells,* and *tulips* tell you.

2 Use the diagram to help you. Which of these sentences would go BEST at the end of the paragraph?

F Her favorite flowers are daisies.

G She planted four kinds of flowers.

H Tulips come in many colors.

J Some bluebells can grow in sand.

Think about the information the diagram gives.

© Harcourt

Name _____

➡️ **Read the paragraph and the diagram. Then choose the best answer to each question.**

Mrs. Jacobs's Garden

Mrs. Jacobs has a large flower garden in her backyard. She is interested in growing plants from seeds. Each part of her garden has one kind of plant.

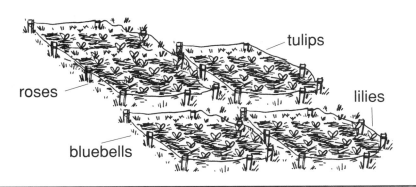

1 **The diagram tells —**

   A   which plants are in the garden.

   B   how long the garden is.

   C   how many years Mrs. Jacobs has gardened.

   D   which plants need more water.

The words in the diagram are called *labels*. Think about the information that the labels give.

2 **Use the diagram to help you. Which of these sentences would go BEST at the end of the paragraph?**

   F   Her favorite flowers are daisies.

   G   She planted four kinds of flowers.

   H   Tulips come in many colors.

   J   Some bluebells can grow in sand.

3 **According to the diagram, Mrs. Jacobs planted more —**

   A   tulips than roses.

   B   lilies than bluebells.

   C   roses than tulips.

   D   bluebells than lilies.

➡️ **Read the paragraph and the diagram. Then choose the best answer to each question.**

Mrs. Jacobs's Garden

Mrs. Jacobs has a large flower garden next to her greenhouse. She is interested in growing plants from seeds. Each section of her garden contains one type of plant.

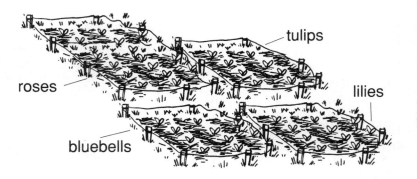

1 The diagram tells —

   A which plants are in the garden.

   B how long the garden is.

   C how many years Mrs. Jacobs has gardened.

   D which plants need more water.

2 Use the diagram to help you. Which of these sentences would go BEST at the end of the paragraph?

   F Her favorite flowers are lilies.

   G She planted four kinds of flowers.

   H Tulips come in many colors.

   J Some bluebells can grow in sand.

3 According to the diagram, Mrs. Jacobs planted more —

   A tulips than roses.

   B lilies than bluebells.

   C roses than tulips.

   D bluebells than lilies.

Name _____ # The Secret Life of Trees

➡ **Look at the books. Then choose the best answer to each question.**

Example: **Which book would you read if you wanted to plant a tree in your yard?**

    A *How a Bush Grows*

    Ⓑ *The ABCs of Planting Trees*

    C *Gina Makes Friends with the Trees*

    D *Trees in Virginia*

1 **Which book would you use if you wanted to write a report about the trees in Virginia?**

    A *How a Bush Grows*

    B *The ABCs of Planting Trees*

    C *Gina Makes Friends with the Trees*

    D *Trees in Virginia*

COACH Tip

A report gives lots of facts. Look for a book title that would have facts about the trees in a state.

2 **Which book probably tells a story?**

    F *How a Bush Grows*

    G *The ABCs of Planting Trees*

    H *Gina Makes Friends with the Trees*

    J *Trees in Virginia*

COACH Tip

Look for the title of a book that could be make-believe.

➡️ **Look at the books. Then choose the best answer to each question.**

1 **Which book would you use if you wanted to write a report about the trees in Virginia?**

   A *How a Bush Grows*

   B *The ABCs of Planting Trees*

   C *Gina Makes Friends with the Trees*

   D *Trees in Virginia*

Tip

Think about which books give facts. Then decide which one would have the most information about the topic of the report.

2 **Which book probably tells a story?**

   F *How a Bush Grows*

   G *The ABCs of Planting Trees*

   H *Gina Makes Friends with the Trees*

   J *Trees in Virginia*

3 **Which book would you read if you wanted to plant a tree in your yard?**

   A *How a Bush Grows*

   B *The ABCs of Planting Trees*

   C *Gina Makes Friends with the Trees*

   D *Trees in Virginia*

© Harcourt

Name _____   **The Secret Life of Trees**

➡ **Look at the books. Then choose the best answer to each question.**

1 Which book would you use if you wanted to write a report about the trees in Virginia?

  A *How a Bush Grows*

  B *The ABCs of Planting Trees*

  C *Gina Makes Friends with the Trees*

  D *Trees in Virginia*

2 Which book probably tells a story?

  F *How a Bush Grows*

  G *The ABCs of Planting Trees*

  H *Gina Makes Friends with the Trees*

  J *Trees in Virginia*

3 Which book would you read if you wanted to plant a tree in your yard?

  A *How a Bush Grows*

  B *The ABCs of Planting Trees*

  C *Gina Makes Friends with the Trees*

  D *Trees in Virginia*

Watermelon Day

➡️ **Read the paragraph. Then choose the best answer to each question.**

A Bug's View

Buster Bug was hot and tired. The sun was right over his head. He had been walking since sunup. He had already passed the tomatoes and peas. Then he saw some big leaves. He stopped to rest. After a few minutes, Buster started walking again. He saw a tall green mountain. It looked like a football with green skin. Buster didn't know if he could reach the top.

Example: **What is the most likely setting for this story?**

    A a grocery store

    Ⓑ a garden

    C near a mountain

    D a football field

> **Coach Tip**
> Think about what the story says and what you know about places where bugs are often found.

1 When does this story likely take place?

    A around sunup

    B around noon

    C around sundown

    D during the night

> **Coach Tip**
> Read the paragraph again to check your answer choice.

2 What do you think Buster hopes to climb?

    F a green pepper

    G a mountain

    H a football

    J a watermelon

© Harcourt

Watermelon Day

➡️ **Read the paragraph. Then choose the best answer to each question.**

A Bug's View

Buster Bug wiped away the sweat. The sun was right over his head. He had been walking since sunup, and he was tired. He had already passed the eggplants and peas. Then he saw some big fuzzy leaves. He stopped to rest in their shade. After fifteen minutes, Buster started walking again. He saw a tall green mountain. It looked kind of like a huge football with green skin. Buster wondered if he could make it to the top.

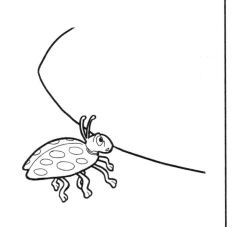

1 What is the most likely setting for this story?

 Tip

Reread the paragraph to get clues about the setting. Use the clues and what you know about bugs to figure out where Buster is.

   A a grocery store

   B a garden

   C near a mountain

   D a football field

2 When does this story likely take place?

   F around sunup

   G around noon

   H around sundown

   J during the night

3 What do you think Buster hopes to climb?

   A a green pepper

   B a mountain

   C a football

   D a watermelon

Read the paragraph. Then choose the best answer to each question.

A Bug's View

Buster Bug wiped his sweaty forehead. The sun was overhead, and he had been walking since sunup. He had already passed the eggplants and peas. Then he saw some leaves that looked like fuzzy green umbrellas. He stopped to rest in their shade. After fifteen minutes, Buster picked up his six feet and marched ahead. A tall green mountain came into view. It was like a huge football with green skin. Buster wondered if he could make it up the slippery slope to the top.

---

1 What is the most likely setting for this story?

   A a grocery store

   B a garden

   C near a mountain

   D a football field

2 When does this story likely take place?

   F around sunup

   G around noon

   H around sundown

   J during the night

3 What do you think Buster hopes to climb?

   A a green pepper

   B a mountain

   C a football

   D a watermelon

Pumpkin Fiesta

➡️ **Think about the rules for adding -s and -es to words. Then choose the word that is spelled correctly.**

Example: berry

    A berrys

    B berryes

    © berries

    D berris

1 branch

    A branchs

    B branchez

    C branchies

    D branches

Tip

Look at the last two letters of the word *branch*. Remember the rule for adding *-es* to words that end in *ch*.

2 field

    F fieldes

    G fieldies

    H fieldds

    J fields

3 puppy

    A puppyes

    B puppies

    C puppes

    D puppys

Tip

Look at the letter before the *y*. Think about the rule for words that end in *y*.

4 buzz

    F buzzes

    G buzzs

    H buzzies

    J buzzys

Pumpkin Fiesta

 Think about the rules for adding -*s* and -*es* to words. Then choose the word that is spelled correctly.

1 branch

   A branchs

   B branchez

   C branchies

   D branches

2 field

   F fieldes

   G fieldies

   H fieldds

   J fields

3 puppy

   A puppyes

   B puppies

   C puppes

   D puppys

 Tip

Look at the letter before *y*. Think about the rule for adding -*es* to a word that ends in a consonant and *y*.

4 buzz

   F buzzes

   G buzzs

   H buzzies

   J buzzys

5 flash

   A flashes

   B flashs

   C flashies

   D flashez

➡️ **Think about the rules for adding -s and -es to words. Then choose the word that is spelled correctly.**

1 branch

- A branchs
- B branchez
- C branchies
- D branches

2 field

- F fieldes
- G fieldies
- H fieldds
- J fields

3 puppy

- A puppyes
- B puppies
- C puppes
- D puppys

4 buzz

- F buzzes
- G buzzs
- H buzzies
- J buzzys

5 flash

- A flashes
- B flashs
- C flashies
- D flashez

6 gorilla

- F gorillaes
- G gorillas
- H gorillies
- J gorilles

7 cry

- A cryes
- B crys
- C cris
- D cries

8 lunch

- F lunchs
- G lunchies
- H lunchis
- J lunches

9 sport

- A sporties
- B sportes
- C sports
- D sportz

10 fox

- F foxes
- G foxs
- H foxies
- J foxxes

Samir wants to write a paragraph that gives information about koalas. He made this K-W-L Chart to help him. Use it to answer questions 1 and 2.

K What I Know	W What I Want to Know	L What I Learned
Koalas look like toy bears. Koalas have soft fur. Koalas are gray or brown.	Are koalas bears? Where do they live? What are baby koalas like? _____	(1) Koalas are part of the same family as kangaroos. (2) Koalas need to live with other koalas. They live in trees. (3) A baby koala is a joey. It is tiny. It lives and grows in its mother's pouch. (4) I have a stuffed toy koala.

1 Which of these does not belong in the <u>What I Learned</u> column?

A   1

B   2

C   3

D   4

2 Which of these could Samir add to his chart under <u>What I Want to Know</u>?

F   Do you like koalas?

G   What do koalas eat?

H   A koala has a shiny black nose.

J   Some koalas live in the zoo.

➡️ **Here is the first part of Samir's draft. Use it to answer questions 3 and 4.**

> (1) Koalas live in trees with other koalas. (2) Most people think koalas are bears, but they not are. (3) They belong to the same family as kangaroos. (4) All mothers in this family have a pouch. (5) I have a lot of stuffed koalas.

3 Which of these sentences does not belong in Samir's paragraph?

   A 2

   B 3

   C 4

   D 5

4 How should sentence 2 be written?

   F Most people think koalas are bears, but they are not.

   G Most people think koalas are bears, But they are not.

   H most people think koalas are bears but not they are.

   J Are koalas people or bears?

5 Which of these could be added before sentence 1 to tell the main idea of the paragraph?

   A My stuffed koala is white and brown.

   B Koalas are interesting animals.

   C Koalas and kangaroos do not look alike.

   D I like animals that jump.

Read the next part of Samir's draft and answer the questions. This part has underlined words. The questions ask about the underlined words.

---

(6) A baby koala is tiny when it is born. (7) <u>It look like</u> a pink jelly bean. (8) Koala <u>babees</u> live and grow in their <u>mother pouches</u>.
(9) A baby koala is called a joey.

---

6 In sentence 7, <u>It look like</u> should be written —

  A it looks like

  B It looks like

  C It look Like

  D it look like

7 In sentence 8, <u>babbes</u> should be written —

  F babys

  G Babees

  H babeis

  J babies

8 In sentence 8, <u>mother pouches</u> should be written —

  A mothers' pouches

  B mother pouches

  C mothers pouche's

  D as it is

➡ **Read the paragraph. Then choose the best answer to each question.**

Doing the Wash

My older brother and I did the wash when Mom was sick. When I took the clothes out of the washer, my white socks were pink. I had put a red shirt in the washer, and the color had run. When I took the clothes out of the dryer, I was shocked. The heat had made my brother's sweatshirt shrink. Now both of us had clothes we could not wear. My brother and I were upset. Doing the wash wasn't as easy as we had thought.

Example: Why didn't Mom do the wash?

   A She had to go to school.

   B The washing machine was broken.

   C It was her birthday.

   Ⓓ She was sick.

1 Why did the white socks turn pink?

   A The color from the red shirt had run.

   B Cold water turned them pink.

   C Other pink clothes turned them pink.

   D The brother had put pink soap in the machine.

Remember that a cause tells *why* something happens.

2 Why were the boy and his older brother upset?

   F They didn't like Mom being sick at home.

   G They didn't like missing a big baseball game.

   H They didn't like having clothes they could not wear.

   J They didn't like hanging out the wash to dry.

Often the cause happens right before the effect.

Read the paragraph. Then choose the best answer to each question.

Doing the Wash

When Mom was sick, my older brother and I did the wash. We washed the light-colored clothes first. When I took the clothes out of the washer, my white socks were pink. I'd put a red shirt in the washer by mistake, and the color had run. When I took the clothes out of the dryer, my brother's sweatshirt had shrunk so much that it would fit a doll. Now both of us had clothes we couldn't wear! My brother and I were upset. Doing laundry wasn't nearly as easy as we had thought.

---

1 Why didn't Mom do the wash?

   A She had to go to school.

   B The washing machine was broken.

   C It was her birthday.

   D She was sick.

Coach Tip

All of these answers could be real causes. Only one of them, however, is found in the story.

2 Why did the white socks turn pink?

   F The color from the red shirt had run.

   G Cold water turned them pink.

   H Other pink clothes turned them pink.

   J The brother had put pink soap in the machine.

3 Why were the boy and his older brother upset?

   A They didn't like Mom being sick at home.

   B They didn't like missing a big baseball game.

   C They didn't like having clothes they could not wear.

   D They didn't like hanging out the wash to dry.

Read the paragraph. Then choose the best answer to each question.

Doing the Wash

Last Saturday, my mom had the flu. My older brother and I offered to wash the clothes. Mom had told us to sort the clothes and do a light-colored load first. When I took the clothes out of the washer, my white socks were pink. I'd put a red shirt in the washer by mistake, and the color had run. When I took the clothes out of the dryer, my brother's sweatshirt had shrunk so much that it would fit a teddy bear. Now both of us had ruined clothes! My brother and I were upset. Doing laundry wasn't nearly as easy as we'd thought it would be.

---

1 Why didn't Mom do the wash?

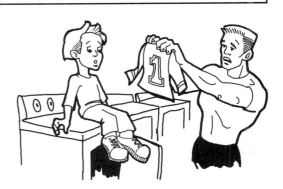

  A She had to go to school.

  B The washing machine was broken.

  C It was her birthday.

  D She was sick.

2 Why did the white socks turn pink?

  F The color from the red shirt had run.

  G Cold water turned them pink.

  H Other pink clothes turned them pink.

  J The brother had put pink soap in the machine.

3 Why were the boy and his older brother upset?

  A They didn't like Mom being sick at home.

  B They didn't like missing a big baseball game.

  C They didn't like having clothes they could not wear.

  D They didn't like hanging out the wash to dry.

© Harcourt

➡️ **Find the word that has the same sound as the underlined letters in the first word.**

Example: cowb<u>oy</u>

    A cowbell

    B away

    C vote

    ⓓ voice

1 sp<u>oi</u>l

    A brown

    B spill

    C boy

    D spot

> COACH **Tip**
> Look at the underlined letters closely. Be sure you know the sound they make.

2 enj<u>oy</u>

    F choice

    G enter

    H joke

    J ending

3 p<u>oi</u>nt

    A poster

    B plant

    C topcoat

    D toybox

> COACH **Tip**
> Remember that the letters *oi* and *oy* can stand for the same vowel sound.

4 v<u>oy</u>age

    F vacation

    G boil

    H boast

    J stage

➡ **Find the word that has the same sound as the underlined letters in the first word.**

1 sp<u>oi</u>l

    A brown

    B spill

    C boy

    D spot

2 enj<u>oy</u>

    F choice

    G enter

    H joke

    J ending

> **COACH** **Tip**
>
> Say each word softly to yourself. Listen for the same vowel sound that you hear in the underlined letters.

3 p<u>oi</u>nt

    A poster

    B plant

    C topcoat

    D toybox

4 v<u>oy</u>age

    F vacation

    G boil

    H boast

    J stage

5 c<u>oi</u>l

    A annoy

    B another

    C call

    D clean

➡ **Find the word that has the same sound as the underlined letters in the first word.**

1 sp<u>oi</u>l

  A brown

  B spill

  C boy

  D spot

2 enj<u>oy</u>

  F choice

  G enter

  H joke

  J ending

3 p<u>oi</u>nt

  A poster

  B plant

  C topcoat

  D toybox

4 v<u>oy</u>age

  F vacation

  G boil

  H boast

  J stage

5 c<u>oi</u>l

  A annoy

  B another

  C call

  D clean

6 l<u>oy</u>al

  F lightly

  G ocean

  H lost

  J oily

7 empl<u>oy</u>er

  A player

  B entrance

  C explode

  D pointer

8 t<u>oy</u>

  F toad

  G toil

  H tone

  J toll

9 v<u>oi</u>ce

  A arrive

  B jumping

  C joyful

  D article

10 n<u>oi</u>se

  F boyhood

  G brother

  H bookmark

  J blackbird

➡ **Read the paragraph. Then choose the best answer to each question.**

The Disappearing Hamburger

Mr. Lewis gave his dog, Muffin, a quick pat. It was Mr. Lewis's turn to cook dinner. His wife would be home at six o'clock. Mr. Lewis found some frozen hamburger wrapped in tinfoil in the freezer. He put it on the counter to thaw. Then he went upstairs to work. When he came back at five-thirty, the hamburger was gone. Muffin looked up and wagged her tail. Then Mr. Lewis saw the foil near Muffin's bed.

Example: Mr. Lewis most likely takes turns cooking dinner with —

Ⓐ his wife.

B his neighbor.

C Muffin.

D his baby.

1 What most likely happened to the hamburger?

A Mr. Lewis threw out the hamburger.

B Mr. Lewis ate the hamburger.

C Mrs. Lewis ate the hamburger.

D Muffin ate the hamburger.

 Tip
Think about the order of events and the characters who were in the kitchen.

2 What do you know about dogs that helps you answer the first question?

F Dogs like to eat uncooked meat.

G Dogs can open the freezer door.

H Dogs are able to sleep during the day.

J Dogs like to wag their tails.

Tip
Think about dogs you have seen and read about.

© Harcourt

Dear Mr. Blueberry

 Read the paragraph. Then choose the best answer to each question.

The Disappearing Hamburger

Mr. Lewis gave his dog, Muffin, a quick pat. It was Mr. Lewis's turn to cook. Dinner had to be ready at six o'clock when his wife got home. Mr. Lewis found some frozen hamburger wrapped in tinfoil in the freezer. He put it on the counter to thaw and went upstairs to work. When he came back at five-thirty, the hamburger was missing. Muffin looked up and wagged her tail. Then Mr. Lewis saw the foil near Muffin's bed.

1 What most likely happened to the hamburger?

A Mr. Lewis threw out the hamburger.

B Mr. Lewis ate the hamburger.

C Mrs. Lewis ate the hamburger.

D Muffin ate the hamburger.

 Tip

Reread the story and look for clues that can help you answer this question.

2 What do you know about dogs that helps you answer the first question?

F Dogs like to eat uncooked meat.

G Dogs can open the freezer door.

H Dogs are able to sleep during the day.

J Dogs like to wag their tails.

3 Which part of the story helped you answer the first question?

A Mr. Lewis got the meat out of the freezer.

B It was Mr. Lewis's turn to cook dinner.

C Mr. Lewis saw tinfoil near Muffin's bed.

D Mr. Lewis went upstairs to correct papers.

Read the paragraph. Then choose the best answer to each question.

The Disappearing Hamburger

Mr. Lewis gave his dog, Muffin, a quick pat. It was Mr. Lewis's turn to cook, and dinner needed to be ready at six o'clock when his wife got home. He looked in the refrigerator. In the back of the freezer, Mr. Lewis discovered some frozen hamburger wrapped in tinfoil. He placed it on the counter to defrost. After giving Muffin another pat, he went upstairs to correct papers. When he came down at five-thirty, the hamburger had disappeared. Muffin looked up and wagged her tail. Then Mr. Lewis spotted the foil on Muffin's cushion.

---

1 What most likely happened to the hamburger?

  A Mr. Lewis threw out the hamburger.

  B Mr. Lewis ate the hamburger.

  C Mrs. Lewis ate the hamburger.

  D Muffin ate the hamburger.

2 What do you know about dogs that helps you answer the first question?

  F Dogs like to eat uncooked meat.

  G Dogs can open the freezer door.

  H Dogs are able to sleep during the day.

  J Dogs like to wag their tails.

3 Which part of the story helped you answer the first question?

  A Mr. Lewis got the meat out of the freezer.

  B It was Mr. Lewis's turn to cook dinner.

  C Mr. Lewis saw tinfoil near Muffin's bed.

  D Mr. Lewis went upstairs to correct papers.

Read the paragraph. Then choose the best answer to each question.

An E-Mail Surprise

Michele <u>opened</u> the e-mail from her grandmother. Grandmother talked about the <u>cold</u> winter weather. She said she was tired of wearing her <u>heavy</u> jacket. Michele looked through some magazines. She found some pictures of beautiful beaches. She scanned the pictures and sent them as a surprise to her grandmother.

Example: Which word is an antonym for <u>cold</u>?

    A dark

    B snowy

    Ⓒ hot

    D slow

---

1 Which word is an antonym for <u>opened</u>?

    A closed

    B emptied

    C received

    D sent

Look for the choice that means the opposite of *opened.*

---

2 Which word is an antonym for <u>heavy</u>?

    F easy

    G warm

    H light

    J sunny

Reread the sentence with *heavy*. Think about the word's meaning before choosing an answer.

© Harcourt

➡️ **Read the paragraph. Then choose the best answer to each question.**

An E-Mail Surprise

Michele <u>opened</u> her e-mail. She had a message from her grandmother in Vermont. Her grandmother said that it had been a long, cold winter. She was tired of wearing her <u>heavy</u> jacket. Michele got a great idea. She looked through a travel magazine. There she found pictures of beautiful beaches. Tall palm trees waved their branches in the <u>breezy</u> air. Michele scanned the pictures and sent them as a surprise to her grandmother.

---

1 Which word is an antonym for <u>opened</u>?

   A closed

   B emptied

   C received

   D sent

2 Which word is an antonym for <u>heavy</u>?

   F easy

   G warm

   H light

   J sunny

3 Which word is an antonym for <u>breezy</u>?

   A windy

   B warm

   C chilly

   D still

> **COACH Tip**
>
> A good test for antonyms is to use each answer choice in the sentence. Look for the choice that makes the sentence have the opposite meaning.

Read the paragraph. Then choose the best answer to each question.

An E-Mail Surprise

Michele clicked on the mailbox and <u>opened</u> her e-mail. Her grandmother had written a message from Vermont. She said that it had been an unusually cold winter. Grandmother was tired of wearing long underwear and her <u>heavy</u> jacket. Michele had a great idea. She scanned magazine pictures of sandy beaches with palm trees waving in the <u>breezy</u> air. Then she attached the pictures to a cheery message and clicked the Send button.

---

1 Which word is an antonym for <u>opened</u>?

  A closed

  B emptied

  C received

  D sent

2 Which word is an antonym for <u>heavy</u>?

  F easy

  G warm

  H light

  J sunny

3 Which word is an antonym for <u>breezy</u>?

  A windy

  B warm

  C chilly

  D still

➡ **Choose the word with *-ing* or *-ly* correctly added.**

Example: quick

    A quickely

    B quickily

    C quickley

    Ⓓ quickly

1 fall _____

    A faleing

    B faling

    C falling

    D faalling

> **COACH Tip**
> Say each answer choice softly to yourself. Which sounds best?

2 hope

    F hopping

    G hoping

    H hopeing

    J hoppeing

3 poor _____

    A poorly

    B poorely

    C poorrly

    D poorley

> **COACH Tip**
> Picture the correct spelling in your mind. Then read the answer choices.

4 warm

    F warmley

    G warmly

    H warmmly

    J warmle

© Harcourt

The Emperor's Egg

➡ **Choose the word with *-ing* or *-ly* correctly added.**

1 fall

    A faleing

    B faling

    C falling

    D faalling

> **COACH Tip**
>
> Think about the rules for adding *-ing*. Then check to see which word looks and sounds right.

2 hope

    F hopping

    G hoping

    H hopeing

    J hoppeing

3 poor

    A poorly

    B poorely

    C poorrly

    D poorley

4 warm

    F warmley

    G warmly

    H warmmly

    J warmle

5 fish

    A fishhing

    B fishshing

    C fising

    D fishing

➡ **Choose the word with *-ing* or *-ly* correctly added.**

1 fall

  A faleing

  B faling

  C falling

  D faalling

2 hope

  F hopping

  G hoping

  H hopeing

  J hoppeing

3 poor

  A poorly

  B poorely

  C poorrly

  D poorley

4 warm

  F warmley

  G warmly

  H warmmly

  J warmle

5 fish

  A fishhing

  B fishshing

  C fising

  D fishing

6 fly

  F flyying

  G fling

  H fliing

  J flying

7 nice

  A nicely

  B nicly

  C nicelee

  D niceley

8 worry

  F worring

  G worryying

  H worrying

  J worriing

9 exact

  A exactly

  B exactley

  C exactlee

  D exactely

10 usual

  F usualee

  G usually

  H usualy

  J usualley

➡ **Ann wants to write a story about herself. She made this chart to help her write the story. Use it to answer questions 1 and 2.**

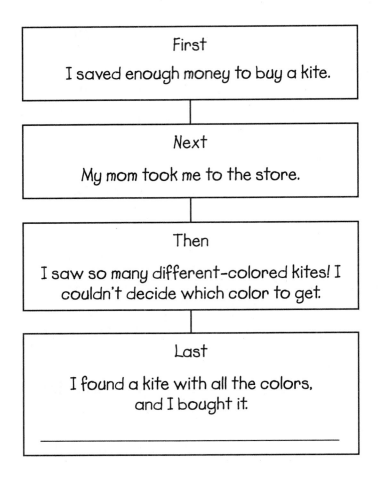

First

I saved enough money to buy a kite.

Next

My mom took me to the store.

Then

I saw so many different-colored kites! I couldn't decide which color to get.

Last

I found a kite with all the colors, and I bought it.

_____

1 This chart will help Ann to —

  A tell her story in an order that makes sense.

  B think of where to fly her kite.

  C tell what she likes about stores.

  D think about how she saved money.

2 Which of these could Ann add to the chart under <u>Last</u>?

  F I wanted to buy a kite.

  G There were red, blue, yellow, and green kites.

  H The kites were different shapes.

  J I flew my kite right away!

Here is the first part of Ann's draft. Use it to answer the questions.

> (1) I had been saving my money to buy a kite. (2) At last I had enough! (3) My mom and I went to the store and we went to the store. (4) When we got there we saw that the shelves were lined with kites. (5) Were kites in every color. (6) I didn't know how I would choose the kite I liked best.

3 Which sentence says the same thing twice?

   A 1

   B 2

   C 3

   D 4

4 Which of the sentences is not a complete sentence?

   F 3

   G 4

   H 5

   J 6

5 Which sentence uses time-order words?

   A 2—At last

   B 4—we saw

   C 5—Were kites

   D 6—liked best

Read the next part of Ann's draft and answer the questions. This part has underlined words. The questions ask about the underlined words.

(7) <u>Then me mom</u> showed me the perfect kite! (8) It had stripes in all the colors. (9) The kite looked like a rainbow. (10) I picked it up and paid the clerk. (11) <u>When i flew my</u> kite, it looked like a rainbow <u>in the skie</u>.

6 **In sentence 7, <u>Then me mom</u> should be written —**

  A Then I mom

  B Then she mom

  C Then her mom

  D Then my mom

7 **In sentence 11, <u>When i flew my</u> should be written —**

  F when I flew my

  G When I flew my

  H When I flew My

  J when I flew My

8 **In sentence 11, <u>in the skie</u> should be written —**

  A in the skigh

  B in the ski

  C in the sky

  D as it is

Name _____

 Read the story. Then choose the best answer to each question.

The Missing Key

Ling was unhappy. She couldn't find her skate key anywhere. She looked in her book bag and desk. She asked her mother and her younger brother. Just then, Wan, her sister, came home. Wan showed Ling the charm bracelet she had made. Ling smiled. Her skate key was on the chain. "You may keep my key if I can wear your bracelet when I go skating."

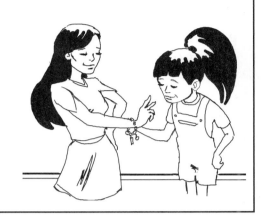

Example: **How does Ling feel at the beginning of the story?**

    Ⓐ unhappy

    B hungry

    C tired

    D bored

1 In this story's plot, what is the problem?

    A Ling wants to make a bracelet.

    B Ling can't find her book bag.

    C Ling can't find her bracelet.

    D Ling can't find her skate key.

The story problem is often found at the beginning of the story.

2 How is the problem solved?

    F Ling finds the key in her book bag.

    G Ling finds the key on her sister's bracelet.

    H Ling's brother tells her that he has the key.

    J Ling finds the key in her desk drawer.

Carefully read each answer choice.

© Harcourt

The Pine Park Mystery

Read the story. Then choose the best answer to each question.

The Missing Key

Ling was upset. She was supposed to meet Amy in fifteen minutes to go skating. She couldn't find her skate key. She looked in her book bag and desk. She asked her mother and her younger brother. Just then, Wan, her older sister, came home. Wan was wearing a bracelet that she had made. Ling's skate key was on the chain. "Nice charm," Ling said. "You can keep my skate key if I can wear the bracelet when I go skating."

---

1 In this story's plot, what is the problem?

  A Ling wants to make a bracelet.

  B Ling can't find her book bag.

  C Ling can't find her bracelet.

  D Ling can't find her skate key.

> **COACH Tip**
>
> Look for a sentence that tells the problem that the most important character in the story must solve.

2 How does Ling deal with the problem?

  F She looks many places for the key.

  G She borrows her friend's skate key.

  H She asks her mother to buy her a new key.

  J She reads a book instead of skating.

3 How is the problem solved?

  A Ling finds the key in her book bag.

  B Ling finds the key on her sister's bracelet.

  C Ling's brother tells her that he has the key.

  D Ling finds the key in her desk drawer.

© Harcourt

➡ **Read the story. Then choose the best answer to each question.**

The Missing Key

Ling was upset. She was supposed to meet Amy in fifteen minutes at the park, but she couldn't find her skate key. She turned her book bag upside down and looked in her desk drawer. She quizzed her mother and her younger brother.

Just as she was about to give up, Wan appeared wearing a charm bracelet that she made in art class. As Ling admired her sister's bracelet, she noticed her skate key on the chain. "Great charm," she said. "You can keep it as long as you'll lend me the bracelet whenever I go skating."

---

1 In this story's plot, what is the problem?

   A Ling wants to make a bracelet.

   B Ling can't find her book bag.

   C Ling can't find her bracelet.

   D Ling can't find her skate key.

2 How does Ling deal with the problem?

   F She looks many places for the key.

   G She borrows her friend's skate key.

   H She asks her mother to buy her a new key.

   J She reads a book instead of skating.

3 How is the problem solved?

   A Ling finds the key in her book bag.

   B Ling finds the key on her sister's bracelet.

   C Ling's brother tells her that he has the key.

   D Ling finds the key in her desk drawer.

© Harcourt

Name _____   **Good-bye, Curtis**

 Choose the word that is the correct contraction for the underlined words.

Example: I am

    A Iam

    Ⓑ I'm

    C I'am

    D Im

1 <u>can not</u>

    A cann't

    B can'nt

    C can't

    D cant

 Tip

To make this contraction, take out two letters and replace them with an apostrophe (').

2 <u>she will</u>

    F she'll

    G she'ill

    H shell

    J she'l

Tip

Skip any choice that does not have an apostrophe.

3 <u>it is</u>

    A itt's

    B it'is

    C its

    D it's

4 <u>have not</u>

    F have'nt

    G haven't

    H havn't

    J havent

➡ **Choose the word that is the correct contraction for the underlined words.**

1 can not

   A cann't

   B can'nt

   C can't

   D cant

2 she will

   F she'll

   G she'ill

   H shell

   J she'l

> **COACH Tip**
>
> Think about rules you know for making contractions. Skip over any choice that does not have an apostrophe.

3 it is

   A itt's

   B it'is

   C its

   D it's

4 have not

   F have'nt

   G haven't

   H havn't

   J havent

5 let us

   A letus

   B let'us

   C let's

   D lets

© Harcourt

Name _____   **Good-bye, Curtis**

➡️ **Choose the word that is the correct contraction for the underlined words.**

1 can not

   A cann't

   B can'nt

   C can't

   D cant

2 she will

   F she'll

   G she'ill

   H shell

   J she'l

3 it is

   A itt's

   B it'is

   C its

   D it's

4 have not

   F have'nt

   G haven't

   H havn't

   J havent

5 let us

   A letus

   B let'us

   C let's

   D lets

6 will not

   F willn't

   G will'nt

   H wolln't

   J won't

7 they will

   A they'll

   B they'ill

   C theyw'll

   D theyll

8 do not

   F donot

   G don't

   H dont

   J do'nt

9 he is

   A heis

   B he'is

   C hes

   D he's

10 they are

   F theyre

   G there

   H they're

   J they'ar

Max Found Two Sticks

 Read the paragraph. Then choose the best answer to each question.

Abe's Favorite Thing

My brother Abe loves to play the drums. He got his first set of drums when he was six. They were a birthday present. The present was from my Uncle Mac. When Abe listens to a tune, he often taps it out on his knees. He also enjoys hitting pots, pans, and pails. When Abe grows up, he hopes to be a drummer in a band.

Example: **In this paragraph, what does the word <u>band</u> mean?**

    A a stripe of color

    B a group of people who play music together

    C a piece of rubber used to hold things together

    D a group of people who live together

1 In this paragraph, what does the word <u>play</u> mean?

    A have fun

    B take part in a game

    C act a part

    D make music on

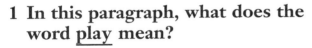

COACH Tip

Find the sentence that has the word *play.* Replace this word with each meaning. Choose the one that makes sense in the paragraph.

2 In this paragraph, what does the word <u>set</u> mean?

    F group of things that match

    G to put in a certain place

    H fixed or already planned

    J the painted background on a stage

COACH Tip

Read each choice carefully. Think about how the word is used in the paragraph.

Name _____

Max Found Two Sticks

➡ **Read the paragraph. Then choose the best answer to each question.**

Abe's Favorite Thing

More than anything, my brother Abe loves to play the drums. He got his first set of drums when he was six. They were a birthday present from my Uncle Mac. Abe listens to music a lot. When he does, he often beats out the rhythm on his knees. Sometimes he enjoys tapping out a tune on pots, pans, or pails. When Abe grows up, he hopes to get a job as a drummer.

---

1 In this paragraph, what does the word <u>play</u> mean?

Rereading the sentences around the word can help you figure out its meaning.

  A have fun

  B take part in a game

  C act a part

  D make music on

2 In this paragraph, what does the word <u>set</u> mean?

  F group of things that match

  G to put in a certain place

  H fixed or already planned

  J the painted background on a stage

3 In this paragraph, what does the word <u>beats</u> mean?

  A mixes or stirs quickly

  B wins against another person or team

  C moves up and down or flaps

  D makes a sound by hitting again and again

Read the paragraph. Then choose the best answer to each question.

Abe's Favorite Thing

More than anything in the world, my brother Abe loves to play the drums. He got his first set of drums when he was just six years old. They were a birthday present from my Uncle Mac. When Abe listens to music on the radio, he often beats out the rhythm on his knees. He'll also play difficult rhythms on pots, pans, pails, and cans. When Abe grows up, he hopes to make drumming his career.

---

1 In this paragraph, what does the word <u>play</u> mean?

  A have fun

  B take part in a game

  C act a part

  D make music on

2 In this paragraph, what does the word <u>set</u> mean?

  F group of things that match

  G to put in a certain place

  H fixed or already planned

  J the painted background on a stage

3 In this paragraph, what does the word <u>beats</u> mean?

  A mixes or stirs quickly

  B wins against another person or team

  C moves up and down or flaps

  D makes a sound by hitting again and again

➡ **Find the word that has the same sound as the underlined letters in the first word.**

Example: graph

    A groom

    B roof

    C teach

    D grass

1 enough ————————————— **Tip**

    A enormous

    B porch

    C please

    D elephant

> Remember that the letters *ph* and *gh* can stand for the "f" sound.

2 telephone ————————————— **Tip**

    F rough

    G rocker

    H polite

    J possible

> Softly say the first word and listen to the sound of the underlined letters. Then read each answer choice and listen for the same sound.

3 tough

    A smooth

    B stiff

    C through

    D toast

4 paragraph

    F laugh

    G plastic

    H painless

    J large

Find the word that has the same sound as the underlined letters in the first word.

1 eno<u>ugh</u>

   A enormous

   B porch

   C please

   D elephant

2 tele<u>ph</u>one

   F rough

   G rocker

   H polite

   J possible

3 to<u>ugh</u>

   A smooth

   B stiff

   C through

   D toast

4 paragra<u>ph</u>

   F laugh

   G parachute

   H painless

   J large

5 cou<u>gh</u>

   A nephew

   B newspaper

   C number

   D napkin

> **COACH Tip**
>
> Say the first word softly to yourself and listen for the sound of the underlined letters. Then say each word choice and listen for the same sound.

Find the word that has the same sound as the underlined letters in the first word.

1 eno<u>ugh</u>

   A enormous

   B porch

   C please

   D elephant

2 telep<u>h</u>one

   F rough

   G rocker

   H polite

   J possible

3 tou<u>gh</u>

   A smooth

   B stiff

   C through

   D toast

4 paragra<u>ph</u>

   F laugh

   G parachute

   H painless

   J large

5 cou<u>gh</u>

   A nephew

   B newspaper

   C number

   D napkin

6 alp<u>h</u>abet

   F anyone

   G replay

   H field

   J drown

7 <u>ph</u>otogra<u>ph</u>

   A potato

   B proud

   C punch

   D proof

8 rou<u>gh</u>ly

   F truth

   G cliff

   H torch

   J company

9 lau<u>gh</u>ter

   A saucepan

   B selfish

   C second

   D seashore

10 dol<u>ph</u>in

   F drama

   G enter

   H draft

   J elbow

➡ **Read the story. Then choose the best answer to each question.**

Autumn in the Country

Last Saturday, my grandparents and I went for a ride in the country. The leaves were beginning to turn colors. The hills were covered with green, red, and gold trees. We stopped at a cider mill and watched the workers press apples. Bees flew around the sweet juice. We bought some cider and pumpkins at the mill before heading home.

Example: **What did the boy and his grandparents buy at the mill?**

    A nuts and pumpkins

    B apples and corn

    C oranges and candy

    Ⓓ cider and pumpkins

1 **What color were the leaves that the boy and his grandparents saw on their ride?**

    A red, purple, and green

    B green, red, and brown

    C green, red, and gold

    D gold, brown, and purple

 Tip
Reread the second and third sentences of the story to find details about the leaves.

2 **Where did the boy and his grandparents stop?**

    F at the top of the hill

    G at a cider mill

    H at a pumpkin patch

    J at a grocery store

 Tip
Reread the story to check your answer choice.

© Harcourt

Read the story. Then choose the best answer to each question.

Autumn in the Country

Last Saturday, my grandparents and I went for a ride in the country. The leaves were beginning to turn colors, and the hillsides had patches of green, red, and gold. We stopped at a cider mill and watched the workers press apples. The smell was delicious. Yellow jackets flew around the sweet, sticky juice. Before we left for home, we bought some cider and a few pumpkins to decorate the porch.

---

1 What color were the leaves that the boy and his grandparents saw on their ride?

  A red, purple, and green

  B green, red, and brown

  C green, red, and gold

  D gold, brown, and purple

 Tip
Think about the color words that give details about the leaves.

2 Where did the boy and his grandparents stop?

  F at the top of the hill

  G at a cider mill

  H at a pumpkin patch

  J at a grocery store

3 What insects were at the cider mill?

  A dragonflies

  B moths and bees

  C ants and flies

  D yellow jackets

Name _____ **Chinatown**

 Read the story. Then choose the best answer to each question.

Autumn in the Country

Last Saturday, my grandparents and I went for a ride in the country. The hillsides were a patchwork of green, red, and gold where the leaves had begun to turn. My grandpa took lots of photos of the beautiful scenery.

Later, we stopped at a cider mill and watched the workers pour baskets of apples into the huge press. Yellow jackets swarmed around the sweet, sticky juice. Before leaving for home, we tasted the cider and bought some huge pumpkins to decorate the porch.

---

1 **What color were the leaves that the boy and his grandparents saw on their ride?**

  A red, purple, and green

  B green, red, and brown

  C green, red, and gold

  D gold, brown, and purple

2 **Where did the boy and his grandparents stop?**

  F at the top of the hill

  G at a cider mill

  H at a pumpkin patch

  J at a grocery store

3 **What insects were at the cider mill?**

  A dragonflies

  B moths and bees

  C ants and flies

  D yellow jackets

➡ **Ramon wants to write paragraphs that describe apple picking. He made this web to help him. Use it to answer questions 1 and 2.**

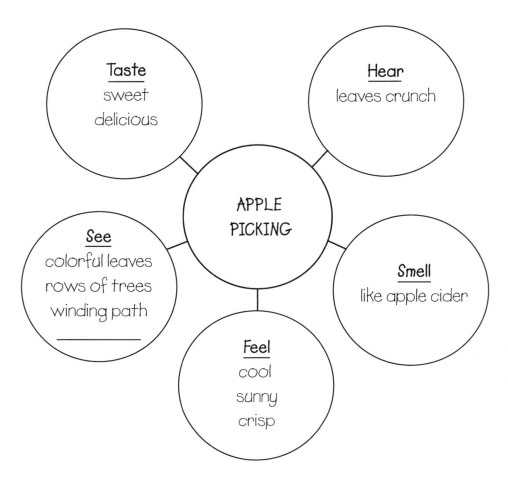

1 Which of these could Ramon add to his web in the blank under <u>See</u>?

  A chilly wind

  B birds chirping

  C apple pie baking

  D bright red apples

2 This web will help Ramon to —

  F plan how to cook apples.

  G tell how to pick apples.

  H think of describing words to use in his paragraphs.

  J write a story about his neighborhood.

Theme 5 Writing

➡️ **Here is the first part of Ramon's draft. Use it to answer the questions.**

---

(1) Today we went apple picking at a nearby farm. (2) It was a cool, sunny day. (3) a crisp day, too. (4) We walked along a narrow, winding path to get to the apple orchard. (5) The leaves were beautiful shades of red, orange, and yellow. (6) We could hear them crunch under our feet as we walked.

---

3 Which of these is not a complete sentence?

   A 3

   B 4

   C 5

   D 6

4 Which of these could be added after sentence 4?

   F We went to a farm to pick apples.

   G This is an interesting paragraph.

   H Beside the path, we saw tall trees with bright leaves.

   J It was a sunny day, but the air was cool and crisp.

5 Which words from the paragraph describe sounds?

   A a cool, sunny day

   B a narrow, winding path

   C beautiful shades of red, orange, and yellow

   D hear them crush

➡ **Read the next part of Ramon's draft and answer the questions. This part has underlined words. The questions ask about the underlined words.**

---

(7) When we got near the orchard, we saw rows and rows of trees filled with bright red apples. (8) The air smelled like apple cider. (9) I plucked an apple off a tree and took a bite. (10) <u>it tasted</u> sweet and delicious. (11) Some of the <u>apples was out</u> of our reach, so we used a long pole to pick them. (12) It was <u>a great day?</u>

---

6 In sentence 10, <u>it tasted</u> should be written —

   A It Tasted

   B It tasteed

   C It tasted

   D as it is

7 In sentence 11, <u>apples was out</u> should be written —

   F apples are out

   G apples were out

   H apples be out

   J apples is out

8 In sentence 12, <u>a great day?</u> should be written —

   A A great day?

   B a great day!

   C A great day.

   D a great day.

Find the word that has the same sound as the underlined letters in the first word.

Example: d<u>are</u>

    A chore

    B chair

    C door

    D date

1 <u>air</u>plane

    A glare

    B around

    C clear

    D party

> **COACH Tip**
> Remember that the letters *air* and *are* can stand for the same sound.

2 comp<u>are</u>d

    F chains

    G chairs

    H completed

    J contest

> **COACH Tip**
> Listen for the sound as you say each answer choice to yourself.

3 p<u>air</u>

    A depart

    B decide

    C deer

    D declare

4 c<u>are</u>ful

    F appear

    G volunteer

    H fairy

    J smarter

Abuela

Find the word that has the same sound as the underlined letters in the first word.

1 <u>ai</u>rplane _____

A glare

B around

C clear

D party

 Tip

Say each word softly to yourself and listen for the sound of the underlined letters. Remember that this sound has different spellings.

2 comp<u>are</u>d

F chains

G chairs

H completed

J contest

3 p<u>air</u>

A depart

B decide

C deer

D declare

4 c<u>are</u>ful

F appear

G volunteer

H fairy

J smarter

5 st<u>air</u>way

A spare

B soapy

C standing

D shine

Find the word that has the same sound as the underlined letters in the first word.

1 airplane

A glare

B around

C clear

D party

2 compared

F chains

G chairs

H completed

J contest

3 pair

A depart

B decide

C deer

D declare

4 careful

F appear

G volunteer

H fairy

J smarter

5 stairway

A spare

B soapy

C standing

D shine

6 dare

F bloom

G bury

H hamster

J hairy

7 repair

A fares

B parties

C fancy

D picture

8 stare

F thanks

G amuse

H airport

J tardy

9 hairbrush

A shaving

B scared

C sharpen

D schoolroom

10 prepared

F freeway

G drawer

H fairground

J dragonfly

Beginner's World Atlas

 Read the table of contents. Then choose the best answer to each question.

Exploring Canada Table of Contents

Chapter 1: Getting Around Canada . . . . page 1

Chapter 2: The Towns and Cities of Canada . . . . page 27

Chapter 3: Canada's National Parks . . . . page 54

Chapter 4: Canadian Festivals and Holidays . . . . page 82

Example: On which page would you begin to find information on Canada's largest national park?

    A page 1

    B page 27

    © page 54

    D page 82

---

1 On which page would you begin to find information on the dates of holidays in Canada?

    A page 1

    B page 27

    C page 54

    D page 82

 Tip

Read each chapter title. Choose the one that tells about holidays in Canada.

2 Which chapter would give you information on the capital city of Canada?

    F Chapter 1

    G Chapter 2

    H Chapter 3

    J Chapter 4

 Tip

Think about the chapter titles. Look for a chapter that tells about cities.

© Harcourt

Read the table of contents. Then choose the best answer to each question.

Exploring Canada **Table of Contents**

1 On which page would you begin to find information on the dates of holidays in Canada?

 Tip

Look for the title of the chapter that you think would include information on this topic.

   A page 1

   B page 27

   C page 54

   D page 82

2 Which chapter would give you information on the capital city of Canada?

   F Chapter 1

   G Chapter 2

   H Chapter 3

   J Chapter 4

3 Which chapter would give you information on train travel in Canada?

   A Chapter 1

   B Chapter 2

   C Chapter 3

   D Chapter 4

Beginner's World Atlas

 Read the table of contents. Then choose the best answer to each question.

Exploring Canada Table of Contents

---

1 On which page would you begin to find information on the dates of holidays in Canada?

   A page 1

   B page 27

   C page 54

   D page 82

2 Which chapter would give you information on the capital city of Canada?

   F Chapter 1

   G Chapter 2

   H Chapter 3

   J Chapter 4

3 Which chapter would give you information on train travel in Canada?

   A Chapter 1

   B Chapter 2

   C Chapter 3

   D Chapter 4

Dinosaurs Travel

➡ **Find the word that has the same sound as the underlined letters in the first word.**

Example: ro̲u̲te

- **A** roast
- **Ⓑ** regroup
- **C** rerun
- **D** grateful

1 yo̲u̲th

- **A** through
- **B** yellow
- **C** those
- **D** yard

 Tip

Remember that the letters *ou* and *ough* can sometimes stand for the same vowel sound.

2 co̲u̲pon

- **F** cabin
- **G** grouped
- **H** grasp
- **J** clapping

 Tip

Say each choice aloud. Listen for the sound of the underlined letters in the first word.

3 thro̲u̲g̲h̲out

- **A** brook
- **B** breakdown
- **C** cougar
- **D** costly

4 ro̲u̲tine

- **F** snowflake
- **G** sudden
- **H** rolling
- **J** soupy

Name _____   **Dinosaurs Travel**

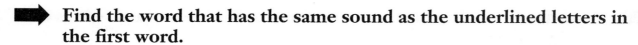

➡ **Find the word that has the same sound as the underlined letters in the first word.**

1 y<u>ou</u>th

   A through

   B yellow

   C those

   D yard

2 c<u>ou</u>pon

   F cabin

   G grouped

   H grasp

   J clapping

3 thr<u>ough</u>out

   A brook

   B breakdown

   C cougar

   D costly

4 r<u>ou</u>tine

   F snowflake

   G sudden

   H rolling

   J soupy

5 y<u>ou</u>'ve

   A throughway

   B throwing

   C shading

   D shouting

COACH Tip

Say the first word softly to yourself and listen for the sound of the underlined letters. Listen for the same sound in each answer choice.

© Harcourt

➡ **Find the word that has the same sound as the underlined letters in the first word.**

1 y<u>ou</u>th

   A through

   B yellow

   C those

   D yard

2 <u>c</u>oupon

   F cabin

   G grouped

   H grasp

   J clapping

3 thr<u>ou</u>ghout

   A brook

   B breakdown

   C cougar

   D costly

4 r<u>ou</u>tine

   F snowflake

   G sudden

   H rolling

   J soupy

5 y<u>ou</u>'ve

   A throughway

   B throwing

   C shading

   D shouting

6 s<u>ou</u>venir

   F stripe

   G thread

   H stronger

   J troupe

7 bay<u>ou</u>

   A forceful

   B youthful

   C fastest

   D youngest

8 thr<u>ough</u>

   F thought

   G throat

   H toucan

   J tomato

9 w<u>ou</u>nded

   A release

   B rabbits

   C regroup

   D returned

10 s<u>ou</u>piest

   F throughout

   G somewhere

   H thorough

   J summertime

Montigue on the High Seas

➡ **Read each sentence. Then choose the correct word to complete the sentence.**

Example: I'll ____ a letter to Grandpa to thank him for the gift.

    A right

    B rite

    Ⓒ write

    D ride

1 I was so hungry that I ate a banana, ____ sandwiches, and four cookies for lunch.

    A two

    B too

    C tool

    D to

> **COACH Tip**
> Use clues in the sentence to help you choose the correct word. How do you write the number 2?

2 The fruit bowl held peaches, apples, oranges, grapes, and ____.

    F pairs

    G parts

    H pares

    J pears

3 The seats over ____ are saved for parents.

    A they're

    B their

    C there

    D than

> **COACH Tip**
> Try to picture the correct answer in your mind.

© Harcourt

Name _____

Montigue on the High Seas

➡ **Read each sentence. Then choose the correct word to complete the sentence.**

1 I was so hungry that I ate a banana,
____ sandwiches, and four cookies for lunch.

COACH Tip

Think about the meaning of each word. Which meaning would make the most sense in this sentence?

    A two

    B too

    C tool

    D to

2 The fruit bowl held peaches, apples,
oranges, grapes, and ____.

    F pairs

    G parts

    H pares

    J pears

3 The seats over ____ are saved for parents.

    A they're

    B their

    C there

    D than

4 I'll ____ a letter to Grandpa to thank him for
the gift.

    F right

    G rite

    H write

    J ride

➡️ **Read each sentence. Then choose the correct word to complete the sentence.**

1 **I was so hungry that I ate a banana, ____ sandwiches, and four cookies for lunch.**

   A two

   B too

   C tool

   D to

2 **The fruit bowl held peaches, apples, oranges, grapes, and ____.**

   F pairs

   G parts

   H pares

   J pears

3 The seats over ____ are saved for parents.

   A they're

   B their

   C there

   D than

4 The cowboy tied the ____ to a post so the horse couldn't run away.

   F raise

   G rains

   H reins

   J reigns

© Harcourt

Name _____

➡ **Read the story. Then choose the best answer for each question.**

Flying Solo

Maria looked out the window of the plane. She was alone in the cockpit. After months of flight school, she was taking her last solo flight. It was the last step before getting her pilot's license.

Maria checked her air speed after looking at her map and compass. Then she looked out the window once more. Ahead was the long runway at Sunnyfield Airport.

---

1 Which sentence would go BEST at the end of the story?

A Maria began to bring the plane in for a landing.

B Maria bought a plane and took her friends for a ride.

C Maria flew to Dayton to see her aunt.

D Maria began to read about how to land an airplane on a runway.

> **Tip**
> Maria has just seen the airport. Think about what pilots do when they approach an airport.

2 The next thing that Maria will do is —

F teach her friends to fly a plane.

G learn to read a compass and a map.

H take photographs of things from the air.

J get her pilot's license.

> **Tip**
> Read all the answer choices. Choose the one that makes the most sense.

Ruth Law Thrills a Nation

➡️ **Read the story. Then choose the best answer for each question.**

Flying Solo

Maria looked at the ground far below. The river looked like a strip of silver ribbon. After months of flight school, she was finally taking her last solo flight. It was the final step before getting her pilot's license.

Maria checked her air speed, the compass, and the map. Then she looked out the window once more. Off in the distance she could see the long concrete runway of Sunnyfield Airport.

---

1 Which sentence would go BEST at the end of the story?

   A   Maria began to bring the plane in for a landing.

   B   Maria bought a plane and took her friends for a ride.

   C   Maria flew to Dayton to see her aunt.

   D   Maria began to read about how to land an airplane on a runway.

> **COACH Tip**
> Think about what is happening in this story. Then try each ending. Choose the one that makes the most sense.

2 The next thing that Maria will do is —

   F   teach her friends to fly a plane.

   G   learn to read a compass and a map.

   H   take photographs of things from the air.

   J   get her pilot's license.

3 Which sentence is a good prediction of what Maria's best friend will say?

   A   "What color airplane will you buy?"

   B   "Congratulations on making your last solo flight!"

   C   "I flew to Florida last week in a big jet."

   D   "Let's take flying lessons together."

Ruth Law Thrills a Nation

➡️ **Read the story. Then choose the best answer for each question.**

Flying Solo

Maria looked at the ground far beneath her. From this height, the fields looked like a checkerboard, and the river sparkled like a silver ribbon. After months of flight school, she was finally taking her last solo flight. It was the final step before getting her pilot's license.

Maria checked her air speed and altitude. After looking at her map and compass, she glanced out the window once more. Off in the distance she could see the long stretch of concrete runway at Sunnyfield Airport.

---

1 Which sentence would go BEST at the end of the story?

  A Maria began to bring the plane in for a landing.

  B Maria bought a plane and took her friends for a ride.

  C Maria flew to Dayton to see her aunt.

  D Maria began to read about how to land an airplane on a runway.

2 The next thing that Maria will do is —

  F teach her friends to fly a plane.

  G learn to read a compass and a map.

  H take photographs of things from the air.

  J get her pilot's license.

3 Which sentence is a good prediction of what Maria's best friend will say?

  A "What color airplane will you buy?"

  B "Congratulations on making your last solo flight!"

  C "I flew to Florida last week in a big jet."

  D "Let's take flying lessons together."

➡ **Lisa wants to write a paragraph that tells how to make pancakes. She made this chart to help her. Use it to answer questions 1 and 2.**

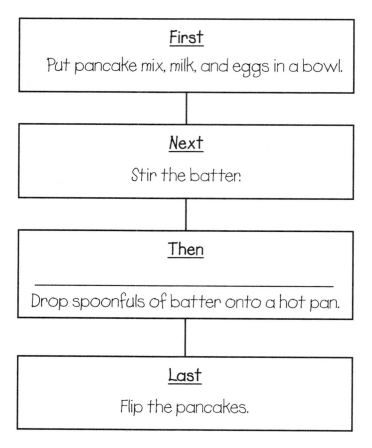

First
Put pancake mix, milk, and eggs in a bowl.

Next
Stir the batter.

Then
_____
Drop spoonfuls of batter onto a hot pan.

Last
Flip the pancakes.

1 This chart will help Lisa to —

  A think about why she likes pancakes.

  B write about eating breakfast.

  C write the steps in the right order.

  D describe how pancakes taste.

2 Which of these could Lisa add to her chart in the blank under <u>Then</u>?

  F Cook them until they are done on both sides.

  G Flip the pancakes.

  H Eat the pancakes.

  J Get an adult to turn on the stove.

© Harcourt

Here is the first part of Lisa's draft. Use it to answer the questions.

---

(1) Every Sunday I help my dad make pancakes. (2) A fun way for us to spend time together. (3) I'll tell you how to do it. (4) You will need pancake mix, milk, eggs, a mixing bowl, a spoon, and a pan. (5) First, put some pancake mix into the bowl and add the milk and eggs. (6) Orange juice is good with pancakes. (7) Next, stir the batter until all the lumps are gone.

---

3 Which of these sentences does not belong in Lisa's paragraph?

   A 1

   B 4

   C 6

   D 7

4 Which of these is not a complete sentence?

   F 1

   G 2

   H 3

   J 5

5 Which sentence has a time-order word?

   A 2—together

   B 3—how

   C 6—good

   D 7—next

Read the next part of Lisa's draft and answer the questions. This part has underlined words. The questions ask about the underlined words.

---

(8) Then, get an adult to light the stove. (9) Carefully drop spoonfuls of batter onto a hot pan. (10) last <u>flip</u> the pancakes when the sides start to turn brown. (11) Eat the pancakes while <u>their</u> hot. (12) I like to eat my pancakes with syrup <u>and froot</u>.

---

6 In sentence 10, <u>last flip the</u> should be written —

  A last, flip the

  B Last, flip the

  C last Flip the

  D Last flip, the

7 In sentence 11, <u>their</u> should be written —

  F they're

  G there

  H they'are

  J as it is

8 In sentence 12, <u>and froot</u> should be written —

  A and frute

  B and fruit

  C and frewt

  D and froote

Practice Test

Practice Test

Bicycles Past and Present

1 Bicycles have changed over the years. The first bicycles were made a long time ago. They had no pedals. A rider sat on a seat and pushed both feet on the ground. The rider was really pushing the bike and making the wheels turn. Old bicycles were made with a large front wheel and a small back wheel. These bicycles were <u>heavy</u>.

2 Modern bicycles are much lighter and <u>easier</u> to ride. They are simpler to ride because they have pedals and the wheels are the same size. Your feet turn the pedals, and the pedals turn the wheels.

3 People ride bicycles everywhere. Some people ride bicycles in the mountains. Other people ride bicycles in races. In many cities, people can ride bicycles to work. Riding a bicycle can be fun.

© Harcourt

1 What is the main idea of this selection?

 A Making a bicycle is hard work.

 B Bicycle safety is important.

 C You should learn to ride a bicycle.

 D Bicycles have changed over the years.

2 How are the first bicycles and modern bicycles different?

 F The first bicycles had no pedals.

 G Modern bicycles are heavier.

 H The first bicycles were faster.

 J The first bicycles were easier to ride.

3 What sentence from the paragraph tells more about the main idea?

 A People should ride bicycles everywhere.

 B Bicycles come in many different colors.

 C Modern bicycles are much lighter and easier to ride.

 D Bicycle riders should wear helmets.

4 Which word means the same as *easier* in paragraph 2?

 F harder

 G simpler

 H taller

 J faster

5 Which word is an antonym for *heavy* in paragraph 1?

 A easy

 B warm

 C light

 D slow

6 What happens when your feet turn bicycle pedals?

 F When your feet turn, the seat moves.

 G When your feet turn, the bike stops.

 H When your feet turn, your feet hurt.

 J When your feet turn, the wheels move.

Read the story. Then answer the questions on the next page.

The New Cat

1 Our family has two pets. We have a gray cat named Molly and a brown dog named Watson. Molly and Watson are friends.

2 One morning my mother opened the kitchen door. A new cat was sitting on the <u>steps</u> outside. I asked our neighbor, Mr. Kramer, if the cat belonged to him.

3 "No, Lizzie, she is not my cat," he said. "I do not think any of the neighbors owns that cat."

4 We named the cat Honey. Mother took Honey to the vet. He said Honey was very healthy. Now all she needed was a home.

5 My family wanted Honey to live in our house. We did not know if Molly and Watson would like her. Mother brought Honey into the kitchen. I called Molly and Watson. First, they all smelled each other. They looked at each other. Then we quietly left the room. We went back later, and all three animals were asleep. I guess the new cat will fit in after all!

© Harcourt

1 In this story's plot, what is the problem?

   A A family wants a new cat to get along with the other family pets.

   B A family lost its cat in the woods.

   C A family lost its cat near the neighborhood park.

   D A family has too many pets and must give away one.

2 Where did Lizzie's mother first see the new cat?

   F The cat was in the backyard.

   G The cat was on the roof.

   H The cat was on the steps outside.

   J The cat was at Mr. Kramer's house.

3 Why do you think Lizzie's mother took Honey to the vet?

   A She wanted to find out who owned Honey.

   B She wanted to make sure Honey was healthy.

   C She wanted to give Honey to the vet.

   D She wanted to buy Honey a toy.

4 What does the family see when they return to the kitchen?

   F The three animals are asleep.

   G The three animals are playing together.

   H The cats have eaten the dog's food.

   J The dog is hiding under the table.

5 In paragraph 2, what does the word *steps* mean?

   A walks

   B a series of actions

   C dance movements

   D stairs

6 Which sentence is a good prediction of what will happen at the end of the story?

   F Lizzie will give the new cat to Mr. Kramer.

   G Lizzie's mother will take the new cat to the vet.

   H The new cat will live with the family.

   J The three pets will not get along.

Practice Test

 Find the word that has the same sound as the underlined letters in the first word.

1 sh<u>ake</u>

   A flame

   B flake

   C frame

   D shop

2 bl<u>ame</u>

   F shake

   G black

   H same

   J bride

3 <u>har</u>mful

   A hearing

   B alarmed

   C bell

   D bare

4 app<u>ear</u>

   F about

   G cheer

   H stare

   J farm

5 ch<u>oi</u>ce

   A enjoy

   B mouse

   C more

   D choose

6 cou<u>gh</u>

   F telephone

   G crack

   H crash

   J temperature

7 b<u>ar</u>ely

   A hard

   B repair

   C replace

   D around

8 <u>through</u>

   F three

   G soupy

   H touch

   J stopped

Find the word in which the letters *ed* have the same sound they have in the first word.

9 picked

   A stayed

   B needed

   C walked

   D waited

Choose the correct abbreviation for each word.

10 foot

   F Ft.

   G FT

   H ft.

   J ft

11 Wednesday

   A Wen.

   B Wed.

   C wed.

   D Wed

Choose the word that is spelled correctly.

12 berry

   F berrys

   G berryes

   H berries

   J berres

Choose the word that is spelled correctly.

13 bake

   A bakeing

   B bakking

   C baking

   D bakkeing

Choose the word that is the correct contraction for the underlined words.

14 <u>can</u> <u>not</u>

   F can'nt

   G cant

   H cann't

   J can't

15 <u>he</u> <u>will</u>

   A he'll

   B he'ill

   C hill

   D he'l

Choose the correct word to complete the sentence.

16 Chase got a new ____ of shoes.

   F pare

   G pair

   H part

   J pear

➡️ **Read the story map that Marco made to help him write a personal story. Use it to answer questions 1, 2, and 3 on the next page.**

My Class Book Sale

Beginning

Everyone brought books to sell.

_____

Middle

Students and parents came.

_____

End

I paid for my books and felt happy.

_____

➡️ **Here is Marco's draft. Use it to answer questions 4, 5, and 6 on the next page.**

(1) <u>Last thursday,</u> my class had a book sale at school. (2) wanted to raise money for the library. (3) Everyone brought books to sell. (4) We set up the books in boxes. (5) Students and parents came. (6) They picked through the boxes and found books they wanted to buy. (7) I found two books I liked one book was about animals. (8) I paid my teacher for the books. (9) I felt happy because I helped the library and got some good books, too.

Practice Test

1 **What will the story map help Marco do?**

   A The map will help Marco tell what kind of books he likes.

   B The map will help Marco tell how he saved money.

   C The map will help Marco tell his story in an order that makes sense.

   D The map will help Marco think about his teacher.

2 **Which of these could Marco add to the map in the blank under Beginning?**

   F We paid for the books.

   G They picked through the boxes.

   H They looked for books to buy.

   J We set up the books in boxes.

3 **Which of these could Marco add to the map in the blank under End?**

   A We gave all the money we raised to the library.

   B Everyone brought books from home.

   C We made signs to advertise the book sale.

   D Everyone picked through the boxes.

4 **Which of these is not a complete sentence?**

   F 2

   G 4

   H 5

   J 8

5 **Which of these is the best way to write sentence 7?**

   A I found two books I liked one book about animals.

   B I found two books I liked. One book was about animals.

   C I found two books I liked or one book was about animals.

   D I found two books. I liked one book was about animals.

6 **In sentence 1, how should Last thursday, be written?**

   F Last Thursday,

   G last thursday,

   H last Thursday

   J Last Thursday?

➡️ **Lindsay wants to write a paragraph that gives information about insects. She made this web to help her. Use it to answer questions 1, 2, and 3 on the next page.**

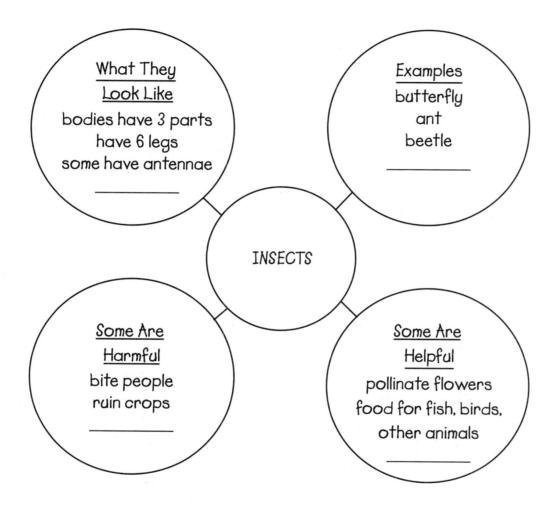

➡️ **Here is Lindsay's draft. Use it to answer questions 4, 5, and 6 on the next page.**

(1) All insects are alike in some ways but not in others. (2) <u>All insects has</u> six legs and three body parts. (3) Some insects have wings and some have antennae. (4) Insects are different colors, sizes, and shapes. (5) <u>Butterflys</u> are insects. (6) So are ants, fleas, and beetles. (7) Some insects are harmful. (8) They can bite people and ruin crops. (9) Some insects are helpful. (10) They pollinate flowers to make food. (11) They are food for fish, birds, and other animals. (12) Some even eat other insects that are harmful.

1 The web will help Lindsay to —

A find out if people like insects.

B plan what to write in her paragraph.

C learn how insects grow.

D learn how to grow an ant farm.

2 Which of these could Lindsay add to the web in the blank under <u>What They Look Like</u>?

F spiders are not insects

G some taste with their feet

H some have wings

J fleas are insects

3 In which circle could Lindsay add "eat harmful insects"?

A What They Look Like

B Examples

C Some Are Helpful

D Some Are Harmful

4 Which sentence tells the main idea of Lindsay's paragraph?

F 1

G 2

H 4

J 7

5 In sentence 2, <u>All insects has</u> should be written —

A all insects have

B All insects had

C All insects have

D all insects has

6 In sentence 5, <u>Butterflys</u> should be written —

F Butterflyes

G Butterflyies

H Butterflis

J Butterflies